George Grimm

The Australian Explorers

Their Labours, Perils, and Achievements

George Grimm

The Australian Explorers
Their Labours, Perils, and Achievements

ISBN/EAN: 9783744778992

Printed in Europe, USA, Canada, Australia, Japan

Cover: Foto ©ninafisch / pixelio.de

More available books at **www.hansebooks.com**

THE
AUSTRALIAN EXPLORERS

THEIR

LABOURS, PERILS, AND ACHIEVEMENTS

BEING A NARRATIVE OF DISCOVERY FROM THE LANDING OF CAPTAIN
COOK TO THE CENTENNIAL YEAR

BY

GEORGE GRIMM, M.A.

MINISTER OF ST. PAUL'S, BALMAIN WEST, SYDNEY; AND TUTOR IN
APOLOGETICS AND SYSTEMATIC THEOLOGY TO THE PRESBY-
TERIAN CHURCH OF NEW SOUTH WALES

GEORGE ROBERTSON & COMPANY
MELBOURNE AND SYDNEY
1888

TO THE MEMORY

OF THE LATE

JOHN DUNMORE LANG, D.D.

IN GRATEFUL REMEMBRANCE

OF MUCH PLEASANT INTERCOURSE

THIS VOLUME IS AFFECTIONATELY INSCRIBED

PREFACE.

THE STORY OF THE EXPLORATION OF AUSTRALIA is one which we cannot willingly let die. There are many reasons for keeping alive the remembrance of such heroic deeds. It is due to the memory of those men who took their lives in their hands, and, in many cases, laid their bones in the desert; it is an act of gratitude on our part, who have entered on their labours; and it is a kind of information indispensable to every Australian who desires to know the history of his country. And yet there is great danger of their being practically forgotten. The time when the harvest of discovery was reaped has faded into the past, and a generation is growing up not well informed on these most interesting adventures and achievements. Nor are the sources of information easily obtainable by those who purposely put themselves on the search. The journals of the explorers, never too plentiful, have now become scarce. They are only occasionally met with in private hands, where they are, for good reasons, held as a treasure. A considerable number of these works are to be found in the Sydney School of Arts, but they have been withdrawn from circulation, and are now kept for special reference only, in a glass case, under lock and key. The

Government Library contains the best collection extant, but even there it has been deemed necessary to adopt restrictive regulations, with the view of giving the books a longer lease of existence. This scarcity of the sources of information, and these restrictions which fence in the few that remain, may be accepted as a sufficient plea for the effort here made to popularize the knowledge they contain. But I would warn the reader not to expect from this small volume what it does not profess to give. In no sense does it pretend to be elaborate or exhaustive. I have had to study brevity for another reason than its being the soul of wit. It would have been a pleasant task to write long descriptions of Australian scenery, and to follow the explorers even into the by-paths of their journeys; but the result would have been just what I have had to avoid—a bulky volume. Yet, such as it is, I hope the book will be found acceptable to the man of business, who can neither afford to be ignorant of this subject nor find time to enter into its minutiæ; to the youth of our country, who cannot obtain access to the original sources; and to the general reader, who desires to be told in simple, artless language the main outlines of this fascinating story.

Having written on a subject in no way connected with my profession, I may be allowed to say, in a word, how my thoughts came to be diverted into this channel. Probably they would never have been so directed to any great extent had it not happened that the path of duty led me into the tracks of several of the most eminent explorers. In earlier days it was my lot to travel, in the service of the Gospel, most extensively in the interior of Queensland, principally on the lines of the Condamine, the Dawson, the Balonne, the Maranoa, and the Warrego rivers. In these situations it was natural to wish for information as to the way and manner in which those pastoral regions had been opened up for settlement. Not much was to be gleaned from the occupants themselves; but it fortunately happened that Sir Thomas Mitchell's journal fell into my hands when amidst the scenes of one of his most splendid discoveries, the Fitzroy Downs, and almost under the shadow of his well-named Mount Abundance. The taste then obtained was sufficient to whet the appetite for more, and the prosecution of this favourite study has issued in what I may be permitted to call a tolerable acquaintance with the exploration of Australia. About seven or eight years ago I wrote a series of papers on this subject for the *Sydney Mail*, bringing the history down to the expedition of Burke and Wills. The proprietors of that journal have kindly permitted me to make use of my former articles in the preparation of this work; but of this permission, for which I would here record my thanks, I have availed myself only to a moderate extent. The whole has been re-written, some inadvertencies have been corrected, and the history in its main outlines brought down to the present time. Although my principal concern has been with the land explorers, I have, in the introduction, given a sketch of the discoveries made on our coasts by the navigators. So much was necessary to the completeness of my plan, and also because the achievements of both to some extent dovetail into one another. In the arrangement of the succeeding chapters I have followed the chronological order, except in a very few cases where a more important principle of classification will be obvious to the reader.

As regards authorities, I have spared no pains to get at the original sources of information, and have succeeded in all but a few unimportant exceptions. In these cases I have derived some help from interviews with surviving relatives of the explorers and several very old colonists. I have also been indebted for further light to works of acknowledged merit which have been for some time before the public—notably, to the Rev. J. E. Tenison Woods's "Exploration of Australia," and to Mr. Howitt's "Discoveries in Australia, Tasmania, and New Zealand." My best acknowledgments are also due to the Honourable P. G. King, Esq., M.L.C., for the excellent notes he has written on the discoveries made by his distinguished father, Admiral King.

That this small volume may be found to afford pleasant and profitable reading is the earnest wish of

THE AUTHOR.

BALMAIN WEST, SYDNEY,
    18*th May*, 1888.

CONTENTS.

	PAGE
INTRODUCTION—THE AUSTRALIAN NAVIGATORS	1

CHAPTER I.
THE PIONEERS OF THE BLUE MOUNTAINS	25

CHAPTER II.
EVANS'S DISCOVERY OF THE LACHLAN AND MACQUARIE	34

CHAPTER III.
OXLEY'S EXPEDITION TO THE LACHLAN AND MACQUARIE	37

CHAPTER IV.
HUME AND HOVELL'S EXPEDITION FROM LAKE GEORGE TO PORT PHILLIP	45

CHAPTER V.
ALLAN CUNNINGHAM'S EXPLORATIONS	53

CHAPTER VI.
CAPTAIN STURT'S THREE EXPEDITIONS	66

CHAPTER VII.
EYRE'S ADVENTUROUS JOURNEY ALONG THE GREAT AUSTRALIAN BIGHT	96

CHAPTER VIII.
SIR THOMAS MITCHELL'S FOUR EXPEDITIONS	110

CHAPTER IX.

Kennedy's Disastrous Expedition to Cape York - PAGE 144

CHAPTER X.

Leichhardt's Expeditions to Port Essington and into the Interior - - - - - 152

CHAPTER XI.

Mr. A. C. Gregory's Expedition to the North-West Interior - - - - - 163

CHAPTER XII.

Burke and Wills's Expedition Across the Australian Continent - - - - 167

CHAPTER XIII.

Search Expeditions in Quest of Burke and Wills - - - - - - 182

CHAPTER XIV.

John M'Douall Stuart's Expeditions in the South, to the Centre, and Across the Continent - 194

CHAPTER XV.

Colonel Warburton's Journey across the Western Interior - - - - - - 210

CHAPTER XVI.

The Hon. John Forrest's Explorations in Western Australia - - - - - - 219

CHAPTER XVII.

Mr. Ernest Giles's Explorations in Central and Western Australia - - - - 228

CHAPTER XVIII.

Other Explorers in Western Australia—Conclusion 237

THE AUSTRALIAN EXPLORERS.

INTRODUCTION: PIONEER NAVIGATORS.

THE eastern coast of New Holland, as Australia was then called, was discovered by Captain Cook, while engaged in the first of his voyages round the world. Leaving Cape Farewell, in New Zealand, on the 13th of March, 1770, and steering a north-westerly course, on the 18th of April he found the new continent rise into view in one of its south-eastern headlands, which was then named Point Hicks, but is now known as Cape Conran, and reckoned within the territory of Victoria. Henceforward the *Endeavour* was navigated along the coast to its most northern limit. In these southern waters no practicable landing-place was observed till Botany Bay was reached. Here the good ship came to anchor, and nearly a week was passed amidst the strangest sights and scenes. This brief interlude being over, the northern voyage was resumed in quest of further discoveries. Scarcely had the Botany Heads faded from the view when another large inlet was sighted from the deck of the vessel, but, unhappily, not visited. The point of observation being miserably inadequate, the great navigator was all unconscious of his being abreast of the finest harbour of the world, and having given it the name of Port Jackson, in honour of a distinguished English friend, held on his course without pause or delay. For a while all went well with the navigator, but in an hour when no danger was expected a cry of "breakers ahead" brought to everyone on board a sense of extreme peril. By dint of the captain's superior seamanship, and his perfect command over the crew, the ship was turned from the rocks in a critical moment, and the expedition rescued from a disastrous termination. The locality of this threatened calamity was marked by a projection of the land, overhung by a conspicuous hill, to which Cook gave the respective names of Point Danger and Mount Warning, positions which the reader will recognize as now forming the coastal boundary between New South Wales and Queensland. But the *Endeavour* was not to finish her voyage without making a still closer acquaintance with misfortune. Having unconsciously approached a hidden danger in the far north, she landed bodily on a reef, and sustained most serious damage. It was only after the sacrifice of much valuable cargo that she could be floated, and then it taxed all the skill of the captain and the utmost energies of his crew to bring her to the nearest anchorage. The port of safety, reached with so much difficulty, proved to be the mouth of a small river, which has since borne the name of the Endeavour.

The repair of the crazy vessel occupied a period of six weeks, during which "Jack ashore" enjoyed rather exciting holidays, making his first acquaintance with the kangaroo and other grotesque oddities of the Australian fauna. Having again put to sea, only one stage more remained, and this over, the great navigator reached Cape York, the extreme northern limit of this new territory. Cook succeeded in his object to a degree that must have surpassed his most sanguine anticipations, and now took care that his labours should not be in vain, but redound to the benefit of his country. All that was wanting was a declaration of ownership, and this he accordingly made on the spot: "As I am now about to quit the eastern coast of New Holland, which I have coasted from 38° latitude to this place, and which I am confident no European has ever seen before, I once more hoist the English colours (although I have already taken possession of the whole eastern coast by the name of New South Wales, from its great similarity to that part of the principality of Wales), in the right of my sovereign, George III., King of Great Britain."

This welcome gift fell into the hands of the nation in a time of need. Transportation to Virginia having come to an end through the revolt of the American colonies, the English gaols were being filled to overflow with criminals, and a new outlet was imperatively required. Somewhere in the world a place had to be found for a penal settlement. The publication of

Cook's discoveries came in the nick of time, and delivered the Government from embarrassment. It was resolved accordingly to establish a crown colony at Botany Bay, which had been fully and only too favourably described by the circumnavigator. On the 18th of March, 1787, a fleet consisting of eleven ships, carrying 757 convicts and 200 soldiers, was despatched under the command of Captain Phillip, a retired military officer. The voyage being somewhat circuitous, its destination was not reached till the 18th of January following. Less than a week sufficed to show that Cook's picture of Botany had more of colour than correctness. The shores were found to be shallow, the roadstead exposed, and the adjacent land ill suited to the purpose in view. Without loss of time, the Governor, with his assistants, proceeded to examine the capabilities of Port Jackson, which had been cursorily seen at a distance by Cook and dismissed in a single sentence of his otherwise copious narrative. The exploration issued in unmeasured satisfaction and surprise. The party returned to the encampment with the tidings of a harbour with a hundred coves, on the ample bosom of which all the navies of Europe might ride at anchor. Orders to decamp were issued forthwith, and the removal of the nascent colony was the work of but a day or two. The spot selected for the permanent home is contiguous to the modern Circular Quay, and was recommended for acceptance by a clear and limpid stream that glided on its course underneath the indigenous copse. The infant colony had its baptism of hardship, but was able to survive the struggle for existence. The inauguration took place on the 7th of February, 1788, when the settlement was formally proclaimed a crown colony, in circumstances of no small state and ceremony.

The passion for discovery soon took possession of the new arrivals, and the adventurous Governor placed himself in the front of this enterprise. To us who live in times when Australia has ceased to be an unknown land, their efforts in this direction may appear to have been small and the results insignificant, but it should not be forgotten that the horizon was at that time the limit of discovery, even in meagre outline, whilst an accurate survey had scarcely proceeded a couple of miles beyond the settlement. On the 2nd of May the Governor and party sailed off in the long-boat for the purpose of exploring Broken Bay, which had been seen and named by Captain Cook, but not entered. It proved to be the entrance to a large river, expanding to an immense width, and abounding in exquisite natural scenery. Having crossed the bar, three distinct divisions of Broken Bay were explored, and to the last of which they gave the name of Pitt Water, in honour of the far-famed English premier. Next year this success was followed up with the exploration of the river (the Hawkesbury) which here enters the sea. Large tracts of rich alluvial land were found on both sides. In a short time hence these fertile flats became the homes of an industrious agricultural population, who frequently saved Sydney from the horrors of famine. This voyage of discovery was continued as far as Richmond Hill (the Kurrajong), from which position the chasm in the mountains was distinctly seen, and the sentries which guard its entrance named the Carmarthen and Lansdown Hills.

It was the exploration of the coast-line, however, that principally engaged the attention of the infant colony, and for this work two men of rare ability stepped to the front. In 1795, just seven years after the foundation of the colony, Captain Hunter, having been appointed Governor in succession to Captain Phillip, arrived in Port Jackson with the *Reliance* and the *Supply*, bringing George Bass as surgeon and Matthew Flinders in the capacity of midshipman. These adventurous and truly kindred spirits lost no time in girding themselves up for the work of discovery. They had been barely a month in the country when the colonists saw them start on their first expedition. Taking only a boy for general service, and embarking in a boat not more than eight feet long—very suitably named the *Tom Thumb*—they sailed round to Botany Bay, thence up George's River, which was now explored for 20 miles beyond what was previously known. The results were, the opening up of much available land and the commencement of a new settlement under the name of Bankstown, which is still retained. But the success attending this adventure was eclipsed by next year's discoveries, which were achieved under similar difficulties. The tiny

Tom Thumb, with its crew of three all told, again left Port Jackson for the purpose of examining a large river which was supposed to enter the ocean to the south of Botany Bay. Having stood out to sea in order to catch the current, the voyagers unwittingly passed the object of their search and were carried far southward. Bad weather now supervened; the little craft was tossed like a cork on the billows, and finally beached in a heavy surf with the loss of many valuables on board. Being now in want of water, the party were compelled to leave the rock-bound coast and steer still further south, in the hope of finding a more favourable locality. Eventually they cast anchor about two miles beyond the present town of Wollongong, in an inlet which, in commemoration of this incident, still bears the name of the Tom Thumb Lagoon. The blacks, it was ascertained, called the district Allourie, which has, doubtless, been transformed into the more euphonious Illawarra. On the homeward voyage Bass and Flinders made a seasonable discovery of a snug little shelter, which they called Providential Cove, but which is now generally known by the native name, Wattamolla. About four miles further north they were fortunate at last in hitting upon the real object of their search. It proved to be a large sheet of water stretching several miles inland, and presented the appearance of a port rather than a river. The natives spoke of it as "Deeban," but it is now called Port Hacking, it is believed in acknowledgment of the services of a pilot of that name. Having accomplished far more than the object they had in view, the daring seamen returned to Sydney Cove, after passing through a succession of perils and privations which give to their narrative the character, not of sober history, but of wild romance.

The next important expedition was carried out under the sole conduct of Bass. On his own petition the Governor furnished him with a whale-boat, carrying a crew of six seamen and provided with supplies for six weeks only. With so slender an equipment this born adventurer sailed from Port Jackson on a voyage of 600 miles, along a little-known and possibly perilous coast. One lovely summer evening, which happened to be the 3rd of December, 1797, the little whaler with its stout-hearted crew bore round the South Head, and bravely turned its prow towards its unknown destination. Scarcely had the familiar landmarks dropped out of sight when the elements engaged in tempestuous fury, and the storm drove the adventurers to seek shelter first at Port Hacking, next at Wattamolla, and again near Cook's Red Point, on the Illawarra coast. The headland, under the lee of which the vessel took refuge, stands a little to the south of Lake Illawarra, and still bears the name of Bass' Point. Not long after the voyage was resumed he discovered the embouchure of a river in an inferior harbour, which he called Shoalhaven, believing it deserved no better name. Jervis Bay was next entered, but this was no discovery, for it had been previously explored by

Lieutenant Bowen, whose name is still preserved in an island lying near the entrance. Bass, however, had the good luck to discover Twofold Bay—a scene of never-failing beauty, and a place of importance in our early history. Passing rapidly southward he rounded Cape Howe, and first noticed the Long Beach, but was unable to identify Point Hicks. He was now 300 miles from Sydney, and whatever remained of the voyage was along an absolutely unknown coast. Some important discoveries were made at various points, but the most valuable portion of his labours was the exploration of Western Port. Here he remained thirteen days, during which this commodious harbour was carefully examined and fully described. A leading object of the voyage had been to settle the question of the suspected insularity of Van Diemen's Land. Bass had really solved the problem without knowing it, for he had passed through the strait which now bears his name. That it was detached from the continent his own bearings rendered almost a certainty. To do more was impossible in the circumstances. He had already been seven weeks from Sydney, which had been left with only six weeks' provisions. These, though eked out by an occasional supply of fish and fowl, were nearly exhausted, and the homeward voyage was made on the shortest course. During an absence of eleven weeks he had examined the coast for 600 miles south of Port Jackson, the latter half of which had been utterly unknown up to the time of this expedition.

There still remains for review another memorable voyage of discovery, undertaken by Bass and Flinders conjointly in the year 1798. The object of this expedition was to demonstrate the existence of the probable strait and the consequent insularity of Van Diemen's land; and the way it was proposed to accomplish this double object was to sail through the channel and circumnavigate the island. Bent on this adventure Bass and Flinders left Sydney Cove on the 7th October, in the *Norfolk*, a good sea-going sloop of 25 tons burthen. The run over the known waters was made purposely in haste, because the time was limited. Their cruise in the channel disclosed a large number of islands, the haunts of myriads of sea-fowl, particularly the sooty petrel, which, though far from savoury, served as an article of food. This strange bird was found, like the rabbit, to burrow in the ground, where it was easily captured in the evening. Flinders says it was simply necessary to thrust in the whole length of the arm into the hole, whence one would be almost certain to bring out a petrel—or a snake. The alternative was not a pleasant one, but the commander had to husband up the provisions and the sailors were not unwilling to run the risk. The circumnavigation of Van Diemen's Land (Tasmania) commenced at the northern point, known as Cape Portland. Nothing specially remarkable occurred till a point was reached which they named Low Head, immediately after which the *Norfolk* entered an arm of the sea more than a mile in width. This appeared to be a discovery of sufficient importance to devote sixteen days to its exploration. It proved to be the embouchure of what is now known as the River Tamar, on which Launceston, the second town of the island, is built. The discoverers sailed up the estuary, following its course for many miles inland. It was found to be alive with aquatic fowls, particularly black swans, sometimes numbering 500 in a flock. This unexpected diversion proved rich sport, and afforded a pleasant interlude to the monotony of life at sea. But the expedition was not for play, but work, and the ship was again upon her course. After a short sail to the westward they found themselves rounding the north-west cape, and with glad hearts could perceive the shore trending away for many a league to the south. The problem was already virtually solved. "Mr. Bass and myself," says Flinders, "hailed it with joy and mutual congratulation, as announcing the completion of our long-wished-for discovery of a passage into the southern Indian Ocean." This fortunate issue of their labours marked an epoch both in the history of discovery and the progress of international commerce. The circuitous route round the south of Van Diemen's Land could henceforth be avoided, and in our day the intervening strait has become the ordinary highway for the Australian trade. It being still deemed advisable to carry out the instructions to the letter, the circumnavigation of the island was prosecuted with varying interest. In the southern parts some valuable discoveries were made, and errors of previous observers corrected. In consequence of unfavourable weather the run along the eastern coast was made for the most part out of sight of land, but on the 6th of January it was found they had completely rounded Van Diemen's Land, and so brought their work to an end. The time allotted for the expedition having also expired, the heroic navigators returned to Sydney, bringing the welcome intelligence that doubt was no longer possible concerning the insularity of Tasmania, and the practicability of the intervening channel as a highway of commerce. The merit of this latter discovery is almost equally due to both navigators, but with a generosity which reflects credit, and is as noble as it is rare, Flinders prevailed on Governor Hunter to call it Bass' Strait.

What had now been done for the island of Van Diemen's Land by Bass and Flinders conjointly was next to be achieved for the continent of Australia by Flinders single-handed. Before his time much had been done in enterprises of discovery on numerous and distant parts of the coast by various commanders and by different nations; but as these efforts had been conducted under no comprehensive plan, there was no continuous line of exploration, and accordingly the discoveries hitherto made were known only as *disjecta membra*, lying at wide intervals in the Southern Ocean; but whether they were the extremities of one and the same continent, or a cluster of sporadic islands, there was not yet sufficient evidence to show.

To settle this question was the true mission of Matthew Flinders, and the method he adopted was to circumnavigate the whole territory, keeping so near the land as to have his eye on the raging surf, except when the darkness of the night and the wildness of the weather rendered this purpose impracticable. On the very day of his death the printing-press issued a record of his labours in a couple of goodly quartos entitled " A Voyage to Terra Australis." This name was proposed for the new country as a fair and likely means of overcoming an acknowledged difficulty. The Dutch had long ago discovered the western coast and called the country New Holland, whereas the English, having performed a similar service for the eastern side, gave the name of New South Wales to this and the parts adjacent. Herein lay the difficulty; to call the whole continent New Holland seemed unfair to the English, whilst it appeared equally unjust to the Dutch to give the entire country the name of New South Wales. Flinders thought Terra Australis would be a reasonable compromise, but added, in an all-important footnote—" Had I permitted myself any innovation upon the original term, it would have been to convert it into AUSTRALIA, as being more agreeable to the ear and an assimilation to the other great portions of the earth." The suggestion was a most fortunate one, in spite of the innovation, and the remark shows that, among other and greater obligations, we are indebted to this navigator for the name of our country.

On the 18th of July, 1801, Flinders sailed from Spithead in the *Investigator* for the circumnavigation of Australia. The continent was first sighted on the 6th of December at the old landmark of the Leeuwin, which had hitherto been believed to be an island, but was now found to be connected with the mainland, and henceforth known as *Cape* Leeuwin. Having visited King George's Sound, the run was next made along the Great Australian Bight to Fowler's Bay and Nuyt's Archipelago. Other navigators had visited this part and examined it with more or less attention. All the knowledge gained in the next stage had the merit of original discoveries. Foremost among these were Spencer and St. Vincent Gulfs, with Yorke Peninsula intervening, and a large island lying nearly opposite. On the latter they found no human inhabitants, but marsupials and seals were seen in prodigious numbers, and hence the explorers gave it the name of Kangaroo Island. Having never met with any of Adam's children till now, the denizens of the island showed no timidity in the presence of the strangers, nor expected any harm; and this indifference was observed to continue much longer with the kangaroos than with the seals. Flinders was of opinion that the kangaroos mistook their visitors for a variety of seals, but the seals soon became too knowing to confound them with kangaroos. A little sharp experience led both classes of animals to regard the intruders as deadly enemies. From that hour confidence departed and fear took its place. Shortly after the navigator left this island a very memorable incident occurred. A sailor from the mast-head reported a white rock in sight. On a nearer view it proved to be the sails of a ship—of all things surely the last to be expected in this unknown quarter of the world. Both vessels met in these strange waters, and then the apparition turned out to be the French ship the *Geographe*, also on a voyage of discovery, under the command of Captain Baudin. The jealous Frenchman ill concealed his vexation on meeting with a rival who had reaped the harvest of discovery over so many leagues of a coast-line which he believed himself to be the first to visit. Nor was jealousy his only or his worst fault. This unscrupulous navigator had the audacity to proceed as an explorer in unknown waters, and lay claim to discoveries which the Englishman had just made. Flinders, on the contrary, acted like the model of integrity which he was. He maintained the right of prior discovery in respect to all the places he had been the first to visit, leaving to Baudin an undisputed claim on such as he had already examined. This is the reason why the names of localities to the westward of this point are predominantly English, while those lying to the east are French. To the place of meeting, as being a sort of double discovery, Flinders gave the name of Encounter Bay. A minute examination of the remaining portions of this coast having been rendered unnecessary, in consequence of Baudin's cruise, Flinders now pushed on to Bass' Strait and entered an inlet which he supposed to be

Western Port. This conjecture turned out to be a mistake, for the place, so far as Flinders was concerned, proved to be a new discovery. Subsequently, however, he ascertained that the inlet had been visited about ten weeks earlier by Lieutenant Murray, who had given it the name of Port Phillip. Perceiving the importance of the place, Flinders wisely devoted one week to the examination of the bay and the exploration of the immediate neighbourhood. Having seen so many capabilities of land and water, he put on record his opinion that "a settlement would probably be made at Port Phillip some time after." This hesitating prophecy was uttered as late as the year 1802, and the locality in question is the site on which the great city of Melbourne now stands, with its population of 300,000 souls! Having again stood out to sea, the *Investigator* was soon abreast of Western Port, the utmost limit of Bass's discoveries, and now the vessel was considered to be in known waters. A direct run was accordingly made for Port Jackson, and Sydney was reached on the 1st of May, 1802.

Philip Gidley King was at that time governor of New South Wales, and Flinders had the good fortune to find in him both the courtesy of a gentleman and the kindness of a friend. Permission having been obtained from the Admiralty, the Governor placed the *Lady Nelson* at the service of the indefatigable navigator, and in every possible way encouraged his enterprise. Being thus supplied with all requisites which the young settlement could furnish, the

Investigator, accompanied by the *Lady Nelson* as tender, resumed the voyage of circumnavigation under promising auspices. Since the time of Cook the north-eastern coast had been visited in various parts by different navigators, but much yet remained to be done before a correct map could be drawn up, and Flinders had it among his instructions to supply the deficiencies of his predecessors wherever that might be possible. Having taken the trouble to find out what portions of the coast Cook had passed in the night, he made it his business to keep a sharp lookout on such localities, and in this way became the discoverer of Curtis Bay and other inlets of considerable importance. He was able also to correct many of Cook's observations, and being provided with better instruments, supplied, in not a few cases, the shortcomings of several other predecessors. But his most valuable services in this quarter were his observations on the Great Barrier Reef, which for more than a thousand miles runs nearly parallel with the northern coast, and had hitherto been viewed as the terror of navigators. To pierce this obstruction and get out into the open sea was an undertaking of so much intricacy that seamen were accustomed to call it " threading the needle." Even Cook, prince of navigators as he was, failed in the attempt. Flinders persevered till he discovered a safe gap in the mighty rampart, and showed succeeding navigators an easy escape from a grave difficulty. An outside course was then followed to the extreme north. Having now passed through the Endeavour Strait, Flinders came to anchor in the Gulf of Carpentaria, where he found a new scene for his energies and a rich field of discovery awaiting him.

The Gulf of Carpentaria had been early visited by the Dutch navigators, but its exploration—if this word could be applied at all—had been conducted in a desultory and piecemeal fashion. Its turn had come at last, and the same painstaking service was to be rendered here which had made the south and eastern coasts so correctly known. Flinders found the gulf defined on the chart by a vague and hesitating coast-line, which turned out, in most cases, to be more imaginary than according to nature, and he left it so accurately described that his successors have been able to add little to his careful investigations. In this patient research four months were consumed, during which period he examined the whole coast from end to end, including Arnheim Bay. The three sea-boards of Australia, south, east, and north, had now been explored in the *Investigator*. It need not, therefore, occasion surprise to hear of her showing signs of decay. This matter had to be attended to before commencing the survey of the western coast, which was meant to be as thorough as that of the other three had been. After making a call at Timor with despatches, a rapid run was made for Port Jackson by the western coast, but out of sight of land. Cape Leeuwin, the point from which the circum-navigation had started, was reached on the 13th of

May, 1803, and thus the heroic undertaking was virtually accomplished. Shipwreck, tragic sufferings, and diabolical treachery cut off the possibility of any further exploration of the western coast by Matthew Flinders.

The work which was thus left imperfect through a long series of misfortunes was afterwards resumed, and very satisfactorily completed, by another distinguished navigator, Captain, and subsequently Admiral King. He played a prominent part in this period of our history, and was much beloved for his sterling qualities both of head and heart. He made four voyages to the western coast, in every one of which excellent service was rendered to the cause of exploration. The following interesting abstract of his discoveries has been kindly furnished by his son, the Hon. P. G. King, M.L.C. :—

" On the 4th of February, 1817, Lieutenant Philip Parker King, of the Royal Navy, the only son of Captain Philip Gidley King, the third Governor of New South Wales, was appointed by the Lords Commissioners of the Admiralty to carry out a survey of the then unexplored parts of the ' coasts of New South Wales,' which comprised from Arnheim Bay, near the western entrance of the Gulf of Carpentaria, westward, and southward as far as the South-West Cape, including the opening or deep bay called Van Diemen's Bay, and the cluster of islands called the Rosemary Islands, and the inlets behind them. He was also to examine the coast between Cape Leeuwin and Cape Gasselin in M. De Freycinet's chart, and to complete the circumnavigation of the 'continent.'

"The Governors of the colony was directed to place at his disposal any suitable vessel for his purpose, and accordingly the *Mermaid*, a cutter recently arrived from India, of 84 tons burden, was placed under his charge. Mr. F. Bedwell and Mr. John Septimus Roe (afterwards Surveyor-General of Western Australia) were his assistants, and Mr. Allan Cunningham, the botanical collector, specially appointed by Sir Joseph Banks, the botanist of Cook's expedition. The chief of the Broken Bay tribe of aborigines, 'Boon-ga-ree,' accompanied the little expedition, and much service was obtained from him in the various interviews with the natives.

"Taking advantage of the westerly monsoon, the *Mermaid* commenced her work, leaving Port Jackson on the 22nd of December, 1817, and, proceeding by Bass' Strait, arrived off the North-West Cape on the 10th of February. The favourable wind lasted till the beginning of March, when the south-east monsoon obliged the vessel to be worked to the eastward, for the purpose of running before it on her work. Having examined the coast and islands as far as Depuch Bay, the survey was resumed at the Goulburn Islands. Port Essington was examined; also, Van Diemen's Gulf and the Alligator River. A survey was made of the northern shore of Melville Island and Apsley Strait, till the 31st of May, when, provisions drawing to an end and water failing, the little vessel stretched across 'the Great Australian Strait' to Timor, and anchored off the Dutch settlement of Coepang on the 4th of June. On the 19th Montebello and Barrow Islands were surveyed. Dysentery now attacked the ship's company, and further work had to be given up for this, Lieutenant King's first voyage, which, lasting 31½ weeks, terminated in his return to Port Jackson on the 29th of July.

"The winds not proving favourable for the passage through Torres Strait by the eastern coast till February in the following year, 1819, a voyage was made in the interval to Van Diemen's Land, and a survey was made of Macquarie Harbour, on the west coast, and a departure was taken for the second voyage on the 8th of May, during which a running survey was made, including an examination of the entrance of Port Macquarie, from the entrance of the inner passage through the Barrier Reefs at Breaksea Spit to the Endeavour River, thence northerly as far as Cape York. A stretch was now made across the Gulf of Carpentaria, and various parts of the coast to the westward were examined, and Cambridge Gulf and Admiralty Gulf were discovered and surveyed. A second visit had to be made to Coepang to obtain supplies, to enable the vessel to return to Port Jackson, where they arrived on the 12th December, after an absence of 35 weeks. During this voyage a survey had been made of 540 miles of the northern coast, in addition to 500 on the previous expedition, as well as on this occasion making a running survey on the eastern coast of 900 miles.

"The third expedition comprised a further survey of the 900 miles just alluded to, and of the north-west coast in various parts. It may be noteworthy that the cutter was rigged on this occasion with rope made in New South Wales from New Zealand flax (*phormium tenax*). The third voyage was completed on the 9th of December, 1820, having occupied a period of 25½ weeks.

"For the fourth voyage it was found necessary to purchase a larger vessel, and, accordingly, Captain King, who had now received his promotion, found himself in command of a brig of 170 tons, which was thereafter called the *Bathurst*. The coast northwards to Torres Strait was further examined. The Mauritius was visited, and the west coast examined from Rottnest Island to the Buccaneers' Archipelago. The *Bathurst* returned to Port Jackson on the 25th of April, 1822, after an absence of 344 days. Captain King was then ordered by the Admiralty to return to England, to prepare his charts and journals for publication.

"It is impossible in such a short *resumé* of his voyages to allude to the numerous and interesting interviews with the aborigines which he fell in with, further than to state that they were always conducted with a desire to establish friendly relations. Captain King's services were approved by the Admiralty, as he was entrusted with another command of two vessels, to survey the southern coasts of South America."

From 1839 to 1845 the survey of the north-western coasts was continued with the *Beagle*, first under the command of Captain Wickham, and subsequently of Lieutenant Stokes. Soon after arriving from England, in the close of 1837, the coast was examined from Roebuck Bay to King's Sound, during which cruise the Fitzroy River was discovered and navigated for 90 miles from its entrance. In another voyage to the north the coast was explored in the vicinity of Port Essington, which was found to be a spacious harbour. Whilst examining Clarence Strait they made the important discovery of the Adelaide River, which was subsequently described by Mr. J. M'Douall Stuart as one of the best possible situations for a new settlement. Port Darwin was also discovered during this voyage. The *Beagle* now proceeded to Cambridge Gulf, and discovered the Victoria and Fitzmaurice Rivers. The former was navigated for 50 miles, and rather hastily described as one of the finest rivers of Australia. The run was now made to Swan River, and thence, after a cruise among the islands, to Port Jackson. In June, 1841, the *Beagle* again left Sydney, to examine the southern coast of the Gulf of Carpentaria. Some important discoveries were made during this cruise. A fine river, which the explorers named the Flinders, was found, and navigated for 30 miles. On the 1st of August they discovered the Albert. Having ascended to a splendid sheet of water, which was named Hope Reach, they found themselves in the midst of enchanting scenery, which Captain Stokes thus describes:—" It was as glorious a prospect as could greet the eye. A magnificent sheet of water lay before us in one unbroken expanse, resembling a smooth translucent lake. Its gentle repose harmonized exquisitely with the slender, motionless boughs of the drooping gums, palms, and acacias that clustered on the banks, and dipped their feathery foliage in the limpid stream that, like a polished mirror, bore within its bosom the image of the graceful vegetation by which it was bordered. The report of our guns, as they dealt destruction among the quails that here abounded, rolled for the first time along the waters of the Albert, breaking in on the hush of stillness that appeared to reign over all like the presence of a spirit. The country which stretched away from either bank was an extensive plain, covered with long, coarse grass, above which was occasionally seen the head of a kangaroo, listening with its acute ear to our approach." It was not possible to ascend much higher than this reach, on account of the fallen timber which blocked the channel. The explorers then landed on immense plains, which, perhaps with too hasty judgment, they named the Plains of Promise. During this voyage they had examined the Gulf coast for 200 miles, making the discovery of twenty inlets and two large rivers.

CHAPTER I.

THE PIONEERS OF THE BLUE MOUNTAINS.

PERSONS who have yet to make their acquaintance with the early history of New South Wales will learn with surprise that the colony had been founded for almost a quarter of a century before the Blue Mountain barrier was crossed. For so long a period it was scarcely possible to proceed more than forty miles from Sydney in any direction. Many a despairing look must those early settlers have cast on the frowning ramparts of the range, which, leaving only a narrow margin between itself and the sea, threatened to convert the cradle of the colony into a Procrustes' bed, to which its dimensions would have to conform in the future, as they had done in the past. This sense of confinement was the harder to bear that it was met with in a land of freedom; and many a time did the caged eagle dash itself with fruitless rage against the bars of its prison. A record of the unsuccessful attempts to get beyond the main range would form a heroic chapter of our history, and one, too, of which we might well feel proud, if there is any truth in the saying that in great undertakings it is glorious even to fail. Within four months after the arrival of the "first fleet" our annals present a picture of Governor Phillip and party struggling laboriously westward to the gorges of the mountains. In 1793 Lieutenant Dawes, with Captains Trench and Paterson, put forth equally persistent, but just as unsuccessful, efforts to scale the sandstone cliffs and reach the interior. During this year, also, H. Hacking, of the *Sirius*, with two companions, penetrated twenty miles into the mountains, passing over eighteen or nineteen ridges or gullies, and returned to the settlement after an absence of seven days. Three years later George Bass, the famous, though unprofessional, navigator and discoverer of the strait which still bears his name, did all that marvels of perseverance could accomplish in the hope of forcing a passage by way of the valley of the Grose. Taking a party on whose courage he could rely, Bass had his feet armed with iron hooks that he might scale the cliffs, after the manner of a spider, and made his men lower him with ropes into the outlying chasms. But it was all in vain. After fifteen days of heroic endeavour, he returned to Sydney, bringing the cold comfort of impossibility of transit. Bass assured his fellow-colonists that a passage over the Blue Mountains did not exist, even for a person on foot. It is possible that this strong statement was disproved almost immediately after. A tradition, not too well authenticated, speaks of a convict of the name of Wilson actually crossing the mountains in 1799. With another advance we get better footing, and read of a Lieutenant Barrellier making a similar attempt, but only to add another name to the list of failures. Two years later an effort of a more promising character was made by a botanist of the name of Cayley, who pushed his way into the heart of the mountains as far as the present Numantia, where he erected a cairn of stones to mark the furthest limit of exploration to the west. He left his rude monument without a name, but Governor Macquarie, in a sportive mood, called it "Cayley's Repulse," and by this brand it is still remembered by old colonists. The late Dr. Lang thus refers to it in his "History":—" The place was pointed out to me by a respectable settler of the Bathurst district on crossing the mountains for the first time in the year 1826. It is certainly a most remarkable locality, nothing being visible in any direction but immense masses of weather-beaten sandstone rocks, towering over each other in all the sublimity of desolation; quite a deep chasm, intersecting a lofty ridge covered with blasted trees, seems to present an insurmountable barrier to all further progress."

At this outpost discovery appears to have stood still for a considerable period. If further attempts were entered on in the succeeding years very little has been said about them. The settlers must have made up their minds for the time being to submit to the inevitable and reconcile themselves to the situation with the best consolation they could find. But a pressing emergency assailed them before long which aroused the slumbering energy and led to another assault on the western ramparts. A continuous drought had succeeded equally disastrous floods in the Hawkesbury. The live stock of the settlement had by this time increased to 65,121 sheep, 21,343 horned cattle, and 1,891 horses, and all these had to be kept during a season of drought on an area of 80 miles by 40, the greater part of which in the best of times was hopelessly sterile. In this trying situation it became very manifest that one of two alternatives had to be faced—either the Blue Mountain barrier must be forced at all hazards and a way found into the interior, or, should this prove to be absolutely impossible, the surplus stock would have to be removed from the colony, if they were not to perish from starvation. The crisis was a serious one, but it happily called forth an effectual remedy. Three most capable men now came to the front to scale the mountain ramparts from which so many assailants had already been cast down; and now, at last, fortune was pleased to smile on the enterprise. The foremost of this memorable trio was Gregory Blaxland, a native of Kent, and born of an old English family in 1779. The second on the expedition was William Lawson, who was formerly lieutenant in the 102nd regiment, but had latterly retired to "Veteran Hall," his own country seat near Prospect. These two leaders, on whom the whole responsibility devolved, were joined by a third person, then wholly unknown, but who afterwards made for himself a name not to be forgotten in New South Wales. This was the embryo patriot and statesman, William Charles Wentworth. Blaxland was now in his 35th year,

Lawson about the same age, but Wentworth was barely out of his 'teens, and professedly joined the expedition in a freak of youthful adventure.

This memorable expedition, consisting of the three parties named, together with four attendants, a few pack horses, and several hunting dogs, left Blaxland's farm, at South Creek, on the 11th of May, 1813. The same afternoon the Nepean was crossed at Emu Ford, and the first encampment made the same evening at the foot of the mountains which had so long marked the western boundary of the settlement. The plan they resolved to follow was to adhere to the dividing ridge or watershed between the Warragumby and Grose Rivers, being careful to head all the tributaries departing to the right or to the left. This determination proved the secret of their ultimate success, and put the explorers in possession of the only key to the situation. Next morning the Emu Plains were left behind and the ascent of the mountains commenced. The high land of Grose Head is noted as being about seven miles to the northeast, and the place where the ascent began must have been considerably to the north of the present Zig-zag, and near the starting point of the original Bathurst-road. Having scaled the steepest part of the ridge, here about 800 feet high, the travellers were careful to head all the watercourses on both sides, in the hope of finding that the highest ground would also be continuous. The first day's progress amounted to a little over three miles, generally in a south-western direction, and the night's encampment was made at the head of a deep gully, where a small supply of water was found in the rock. Next morning a start was made about 9 o'clock. After proceeding about a mile they had the good luck to hit upon a large tract of forest land. Here was discovered the track of a European, who had marked the trees. This belt of open country ceased about two miles ahead, at which point further progress was obstructed by impenetrable brushwood. The remainder of the day having been consumed in fruitless efforts to round this obstacle, the night was spent in the former position. Next morning the axes were early at work hewing a track through the scrub, which could neither be avoided nor penetrated. This step-by-step progress had to be endured for five miles, until a more open patch was reached. Nor was this an exceptional case. A great part of the route over the mountains had in like manner to be laid open by the axe, thus making it necessary to travel three times over the same ground. First, the track had to be cut out; next, they had to return for the horses; and then the real advance was made for another stage. On the fifth day the brushwood proved so formidable that their progress did not exceed two miles. The following day was Sunday, and the explorers enjoyed the Sabbath rest as much as any toil-worn slave that ever breathed. On the 17th the horses were loaded with a supply of grass, as the country was becoming still more inhospitable, and an advance of seven miles was made through a track which the axe had laid open. But the windings of the watershed now appeared interminable, and the real progress, if measured in a straight line, was small indeed. Yet it was only by this tedious course that the mountains could be crossed, if crossed at all. The locality of the next encampment was destitute of water, and what could be obtained in the vicinity had to be carried up a precipitous cliff 600 feet in height. The horses had to shift as they best could for that evening. To aggravate matters, if such a thing were possible, a more serious obstacle now rose in front of the intrepid explorers. The ridge, which was their only hope, contracted to a width of 20 feet, and appeared to terminate in a huge rock rising 30 feet directly in front. But perseverance, which overcomes all things, brought them safely over this barrier too. Wednesday, the 19th, was a red-letter day, for they now reached the summit of the second elevation of the main range. The site also was suitable for a camp, and offered a good supply of grass and water. Next day a five-mile stage was accomplished, and the camp formed on the margin of a lagoon with a small stream of water running through it. Here the horses were left till the men had cut another day's march through the scrub. Soon after the ridge began to widen, but proved to be more rocky than ever. From the 22nd to the 28th the advance was made at much the same rate and without any incidents calling for particular remark. At last the pioneers had the inexpressible satisfaction of finding themselves on the western fall of the mountains. But the slopes facing the interior were exceedingly rugged, and a practicable descent was nearly despaired of. After much difficulty a barely feasible one was discovered, by means of which the party got clear of the mountains and found themselves in a lovely valley, afterwards called the Vale of Clwydd, and now well known as the site of the town of Hartley.

Now, at last, the Blue Mountains had been crossed, but the pioneers continued their journey a short distance further, to make sure that every obstacle had been overcome. After leaving the range they advanced two miles to the westward on the same day, and encamped on the bank of a fine stream, probably what was afterwards known as the Rivulet, and now, by an absurd blunder in spelling, the River Lett. The last encampment was made on another brook, since called Farmer's Creek, but not from any connection with the farming interest. Here Sir Thomas Mitchell lost his favourite horse "Farmer," and considered the event of sufficient importance to have its remembrance preserved in the name of the creek. From this outpost of the expedition Blaxland went forth on the last afternoon of May, 1813, and ascended a neighbouring hill, from the top of which he beheld a magnificent expanse of pastoral country, sufficient, in his reckoning, to meet the wants of the colony for thirty years to come. This being the extreme point reached in this enterprise, Governor Macquarie paid the leader a well-merited compliment in associating the name of Blaxland with this memorable peak.

The object of the journey being now happily attained, it was judged unnecessary to travel further. Twenty days had been spent in forcing a passage through the formidable mountain barrier, and the progress had been so slow that not much more than three miles per day had been averaged. The actual distance travelled along this tortuous ridge was reckoned at fifty miles, and eight more had been added on the other side. The return journey calls for no detailed remarks. The explorers were greatly fatigued, in very poor health, and their clothes had been torn to rags. Their outward track had been too laboriously hewn through the brushwood to be difficult to find on their return. The colonists at Sydney hailed with welcome the tidings of this signal success, and lost no time in turning the wished-for discovery to practical account.

CHAPTER II.

SURVEYOR EVANS'S DISCOVERY OF THE LACHLAN AND MACQUARIE RIVERS AND THE BATHURST PLAINS.

DELIGHTED with the success which had rewarded the Blue Mountain enterprise, Governor Macquarie took prompt action in following up this conquest over nature's barrier. A new and very capable man was now ready to enter the field. This was Mr. George W. Evans, who at that time filled the office of Deputy-Surveyor. His name occupies an honourable place in our early annals. It were to be wished we had fuller particulars of this first effort of his in the exploration of the colony than are now to hand. The following brief sketch embodies all that is really known on this subject:—He was absent only seven weeks on his first journey, and in 21 days had penetrated 98 miles beyond the most advanced camp of his predecessors. This new explorer crossed the Nepean at Emu Ford on the 20th of November, 1813, and, six days after, arrived at the termination of the journey of the Blue Mountain pioneers. Proceeding westward, he crossed a well-grassed but broken and rugged country, which was subsequently called the Clarence Hilly Range. By the 30th he had reached the dividing ridge which forms the watershed between the eastern and western streams. Soon after this he discovered, in a well-grassed valley, the head waters of a stream that abounded in fish, and hence received the name of the Fish River. He continued to trace it, winding its course through a fine country, suitable for agricultural and grazing purposes, till the 7th of December, when it was joined by another stream, which he named the Campbell. To the river which was thus formed by these tributaries he gave the name of the Macquarie, after the Governor, but the natives called it the Wambool. Continuing on the lead of the Macquarie, he followed it through rich alluvial land—the Bathurst Plains—destitute of timber, but abounding in game. During the whole journey Evans met with only six natives, but saw the smoke of their encampments in many places. He returned to Sydney on the 8th of January, 1814. After a short interval he was again sent out to the same district, with a small party and one month's provisions. During this second journey Limestone Creek was discovered and explored; but its chief result was the discovery of another large river, which he called the Lachlan, after the christian name of the Governor. The Lachlan and the Macquarie formed an enigma to the early geographers. Their sources were in the same neighbourhood, but both flowed towards the interior and kept diverging from one another during every mile of their known course.

The proper sequel to Evans's discoveries was the formation of a road over the mountains to Bathurst Plains. This was done in the same year by gangs of convicts under the command of one Cox, in an incredibly short space of time, as tradition reports. This road, 100 miles in length, was formally opened in May, 1815, by the Governor and Mrs. Macquarie, who rode the whole distance on horseback. Bathurst was then laid out, and has ever since continued to be one of the most flourishing places in the colony, as might well be expected from a town which commands 50,000 acres of first-class land within a radius of ten miles.

CHAPTER III.

OXLEY'S EXPEDITIONS TO THE LACHLAN AND MACQUARIE RIVERS.

THE passion for exploration was not yet allowed to slumber. Deputy-Surveyor Evans's discovery of the Bathurst Plains, with two promising rivers, only whetted the desire for further knowledge. It was presumed that the Lachlan and the Macquarie united their waters in some part of their course and finally disembogued in an unknown part of the eastern coast. But all this was mere conjecture, which required to be cleared up by actual exploration. A new expedition was accordingly set on foot by the Governor, and a fit person appointed to the post of leader. This was the Surveyor-General, John Oxley, R.N., who appears to have been both an able and amiable man, combining the *fortiter in re* with the *suaviter in modo*. Allan Cunningham, who was his close associate, always spoke of Oxley in terms of admiration and endearment. Among other meritorious services he had the credit of giving to New South Wales the first map of her immense territories, a task for which he was well qualified by extensive colonial travel in his official capacity.

I.

This expedition, as finally organized under the conduct of Oxley, consisted of Allan Cunningham, as king's botanist, Charles Frazer, as colonial botanist, William Parr, as mineralogist, and eight others. On the 20th of April, 1817, all the members of the expedition met at a store depôt on the bank of the Lachlan River, which had been fixed as the point of departure. The details of their weary wanderings have been recorded only at too great length in Oxley's published journals. The author in the commencement of his work apologized for the uneventful character of the narrative, and if this was necessary when enthusiasm for exploration was at fever heat, the reader of the present day is not likely to consider it superfluous. The fault, however, did not lie with the writer, but is to be attributed to the uninteresting materials which form the staple of his bulky volumes. The country he had to traverse soon turned out to be singularly tame and tedious. The sea coast, with its never-ending scenes of beauty, had been left far behind ; the mountain ranges, with their vast and varied grandeur, had sunk below the horizon, and in place of both were found only the dull and dreary plains of the Australian bush. Were it not that the whole of the country was new, this record of daily travel would read like the diary of a conscientious but uneventful life. It will be desirable, therefore, to touch only on the chief points of the narrative.

Starting from the point previously indicated, the party proceeded on their travels along the southern bank of the river. Wild fowl appeared in large numbers, offering excellent sport. The natives also were met with more frequently than would have been agreeable had they been disposed to be troublesome, which, fortunately, they were not. The one thing which surprised the explorers was the behaviour of the Lachlan, which, after showing itself a goodly river of a hundred feet in width, threatened to end its career in a most undignified fashion. This it very soon did, as they believed, by resolving itself into a succession of marshes, to which they gave the name of the Lachlan Swamps. Being unable to trace the river any further, Oxley now resolved to abandon the enterprise and return home by a different route. He made up his mind, accordingly, to make for the southern coast, which he hoped to strike about Cape Northumberland, and thence reach Sydney by sea. In this direction the course was steered till the 4th of July, when further progress became extremely difficult, from the sterility of the country and almost interminable forests of mallee, which Oxley, in a play of the imagination, named the Euryalean scrub. At last it became apparent to all that they would have to return to the Lachlan, through the want of water, if for no other cause, and this was now done. The retrograde movement was singularly unfortunate. Had they proceeded only twenty miles further the Murrumbidgee would have been discovered, with its never-failing volume of water. But, in their ignorance, it was otherwise determined, and a laurel lost to the wreath of this distinguished explorer. Nineteen weary days were consumed on this return journey, at the end of which the Lachlan was reached, a long distance below the swamps from which it had emerged, and was flowing in a strong current confined within high banks. Waterfowl were again seen and caught in abundance. Fish also were plentiful, some of them—the "Murray cod"—weighing sixty or seventy pounds. This good fortune induced the explorers to continue their journey down the river, in the hope of reaching some satisfactory result. This expectation was not realized. They were again landed among swamps and marshes, which were now regarded for certain as the termination of the Lachlan, and the exploration was conducted no further in this direction. Here, for the second time, Oxley narrowly missed discovering the Murrumbidgee, from which he was distant not more than two days' journey. The Lachlan had now been followed for about 500 miles from the place where the expedition had started, and it was resolved to proceed no further. A return was now made to Bathurst in an oblique direction, with the intention of striking the Macquarie at a point considerably below the place where it had first been seen by Evans. Some important discoveries were made during this cross-country cut. The Elizabeth River, Bell's River, and the Rivulet were met with and named. Most important of all was the discovery of Wellington Valley, an extensive tract of the finest country, well suited to all the purposes of civilized man, and diversified with scenery of great beauty. After travelling 150 miles from the lower swamps of the Lachlan the Macquarie was struck about 50 miles below the place where it had been seen by Evans. It was a river of good promise, and Oxley was strongly inclined to follow it, as he had done the Lachlan, but the slender remnant of provisions forbade the attempt. The expedition, therefore, made for Bathurst, which was reached on the 29th of August, after an absence of nineteen weeks. The distance travelled from start to finish amounted to 1,200 miles.

II.

Undeterred by the difficulties incurred on the Lachlan, Oxley, during the following year (1818), engaged in a similar expedition for the exploration of the lower course of the Macquarie. Tracing the unknown stream to the westward, he found himself led out of the region of hills into a country presenting a dead and monotonous level. Here the river began to lose its well-defined course and to spread its waters over the dreary expanse. With great difficulty, he succeeded in distinguishing the river from the lake for a short distance onward, after which further effort in a wide waste of water was to no purpose. Now, at last, he lost sight of land and trees altogether, though again able to discern the current of the Macquarie in a stream three feet deep winding in and out among thickets of reeds, which here grew to a gigantic height. Oxley conjectured he had now reached the commencement of an inland sea—a phantom which long played fast and loose with those who loved to speculate on the mysterious regions of Central Australia. In this pet fancy the explorer, like many other theorists, was quite mistaken, for this delusive expanse of water was not even the termination of the Macquarie River. Ten years later Captain Sturt succeeded in tracing it for 66 miles further, and found it ending its dubious career in the River Darling.

Two courses were now open to the expedition—either to return home disappointed, or strike out in a new direction and make fresh discoveries. The latter alternative was adopted. During an earlier part of the journey their attention had been drawn to a lofty range of dark mountains lying athwart the northern horizon. The march was now towards this prominent landmark of the unknown domain of nature. Before it was reached, and after the expedition had been out for about two months, progress was arrested by the discovery of a river running in high flood. This was named the Castlereagh, and a safe passage was obtained after a short delay. There remained a weary journey to the range which had so long loomed in the distance, and was reached after much difficulty, owing to the boggy character of the ground. One of the principal elevations was ascended, from which a magnificent prospect was obtained, and the height ascertained to be about 3,000 feet. Oxley gave to this chain the name of the Arbuthnot Range, but it is still most generally known as the Warrambungle Mountains. The course of the expedition was now directed toward the east, in the hope of ultimately reaching the coast somewhere northward of Sydney. This purpose was rewarded by the discovery of the Liverpool Plains, the most valuable find that had hitherto fallen to the lot of any explorer. This is a splendid area of first-class land, consisting of level country embracing about 17,000 square miles, supposed to have formed in past ages the bed of a small inland sea. The next discovery was the Namoi River, called after Sir Robert Peel by Oxley, but it is still best known under the native designation. After traversing the Liverpool Plains the expedition entered upon the very dissimilar New England country, and experienced fatiguing travel in mountain ranges, which was rewarded by the discovery of another river, named the Apsley. One of the loftiest peaks in this region was ascended by Oxley, and found to be about 6,000 feet in height. From the crown of this mountain giant he was gratified with a glimpse of the Pacific Ocean, and very fittingly gave to his position the name of Mount Seaview. Shortly after the descent from this monarch of the mountains another important river was met with. Oxley called it the Hastings, in memory of the notorious Governor-General of India, and here, for once, the name has stuck. This river was now followed to the sea and the entrance named Port Macquarie, hitherto unknown to Europeans. The exploring party, having now done their work so well, resolved to make for home by travelling along the coast. Difficulties undreamt of were encountered in the indentation of the shore and the estuaries of the rivers, one of which, the Manning, was now first discovered. These obstacles might well have proved insuperable but for their good luck in meeting with a boat, probably the relic of a wreck, which was stranded and half-buried in the sand. The welcome treasure was carried on their shoulders for 90 miles, and put to use in crossing estuaries as they came in the way. With this unexpected help in time of need the party were enabled to reach Port Stephens. This harbour had been discovered by Surveyor Grimes and was now well known. Thence conveyance was obtained by sea to Newcastle, where the toil-worn adventurers found themseves once more within the pale of civilization.

CHAPTER IV.

HUME AND HOVELL'S EXPEDITION FROM LAKE GEORGE TO PORT PHILLIP.

SIR Thomas Brisbane succeeded to the Government of New South Wales on the 1st of December, 1821. The work of exploration, which had received such extraordinary impulse under Macquarie, was taken up with corresponding zeal by the new Governor. The southern limit of discovery at this period stood somewhere about Lake George; and public attention was largely directed to the unknown country lying beyond this outpost. The passion for exploration in this quarter had been discouraged, but not suppressed, by a rash and unwarranted statement made by Oxley in the journal he had given to the world. "We had demonstrated beyond a doubt," said he, "that no river could fall into the sea between Cape Otway and Spencer's Gulf—at least, none deriving its waters from the eastern coast—and that the country south of the parallel of 34 deg., and west of the meridian 147 deg. 30 min. was uninhabitable and useless for all the purposes of civilized man." This singularly unfortunate assertion should have been affirmative instead of negative, for the principal rivers of the continent enter the sea within the limits here specified, and some of the largest tracts of good land in Australia are enclosed by these lines of longitude and latitude.

Governor Brisbane, fortunately, was not convinced by this so-called demonstration, and felt disposed to have the question practically tested. With this object in view, he proposed to the late Alexander Berry, himself no mean explorer, to land a small party of convicts at Cape Howe or Wilson's Promontory, with instructions, under promise of reward, to find their way overland to Lake George as they best could, and ultimately to Sydney. Mr. Berry cordially fell in with the proposal, and recommended as leader of the party a young man who had already made his mark as a bushman. The latter, however, demurred to the plan of the expedition, wishing it to start from Lake George and work its way overland to Western Port, in Bass' Strait. This suggestion was adopted without scruple or delay, and the offer of his services gladly accepted.

This young man's name was Hamilton Hume. He was a native of the colony, having been born at Parramatta in 1797. In those early days educational facilities were few, and it fell out from this cause that Hume owed all the learning he possessed to the instructions of his kind mother. In after life he was more indebted to his instincts than to his education. A bushman, like a poet, is born, not made; and Hume, before leaving his 'teens, proved that genius for exploration was part of his nature. In company with his brother, and when but fifteen years of age, he discovered the district of Berrima, and shortly after completely explored that part of the country. In

1817 he passed the southern boundary of the known territory, and, in conjunction with Surveyor Meehan, made the discovery of Lake Bathurst and the Goulburn Plains. Again, in the year 1821, he proceeded further out, along with several mates, and came upon the Yass Plains. All these discoveries, however valuable for stockholders, may be regarded as but tentative essays in the work of exploration in comparison with what was to follow; yet they must have been highly advantageous in qualifying Hume for the arduous expedition on which his fame must chiefly rest.

While the necessary preparations for this undertaking were afoot, Mr. Berry intimated to the Governor that another person was desirous of being associated with Hume in the position of leader. This was Captain Hovell, of Minto, a retired shipmaster. Having been a professional navigator, he was presumed to be able to reckon longitude and latitude, an accomplishment which the defectively-educated Hume, with all his bushmanship, did not possess. The two men being thus furnished with complementary qualifications, their association in the conduct of the expedition was counted as a certain advantage. This was surely a reasonable expectation; but the event proved that a greater mistake could not have been made. The two leaders, like jealous rivals, quarrelled from the start, kept wrangling throughout the expedition, and, after it was over, maintained a bitter feud, till death put an end to their animosity. The principal share in this work, and credit for the results, have been claimed by both, and it is not easy to satisfy oneself as to the real merits of the case. All things considered, the balance of evidence is in favour of Hume, and he shall have the more prominent place in the following sketch of the expedition.

However favourable the Government might be to the progress of discovery, a poor provision was made for this long and perilous journey. The chief burden of the equipment fell upon the explorers themselves, who were ill able to bear the strain. Hume keenly felt the sacrifice of a favourite iron plough in order to purchase supplies. One way or other, a tolerable provision was forthcoming; and then the explorers, accompanied by six servants, started on the pioneer journey on the 17th of October, 1824. At the close of the first day's march they encamped on the bank of a river near the site of the present town of Yass. From the 19th to the 22nd the expedition was detained in its progress by the Murrumbidgee. In the preceding year this river had been first seen by Europeans in its upper course in the Monaro country; but for all that Hume had virtually the merit of being the discoverer. The Murrumbidgee was found to be in high flood, and threatened an effectual bar to further progress. But difficulty aroused this explorer to Herculean effort. Being supplied with a provision-cart, Hume took off the wheels, and, with the help of a tarpaulin, improvised it into a rough-and-ready punt, which, assisted by one of the men, he dragged across the swollen river. Another day's march brought them to the Narrengullen Meadows, where the party encamped for two nights. Again proceeding southward, the Tumut River was discovered, and crossed without difficulty. Soon after, the expedition was saluted by a splendid surprise. From the summit of a ridge, a little before noon on a clear and beautiful day, the magnificent amphitheatre of the Australian Alps, robed in snow, burst upon the view, and was now first seen by civilized men. About this time, or shortly before, it became evident to Hume that it would be necessary to direct the line of march more to the west, in order to avoid the Snowy Mountains. From this proposal Hovell dissented. Both leaders continued obstinate, and each persisted in following a different course with his respective adherents. A division of property had now become inevitable, and the principle of partition seems to have been that primitive one in virtue of which the stronger gets the larger share. There being only one frying-pan remaining, each of the stalwart leaders simultaneously caught hold of this handy domestic article, and the poor pan went to pieces in the struggle, the result being such as would have followed the adoption of Solomon's advice to halve the living child. The separation of the leaders was not so irremediable as the division of the frying-pan. Hovell soon discovered the folly of schism, and, better thoughts prevailing, returned to re-unite his party with Hume's.

After this incident nothing calling for special mention occurred till the 16th of November, which was signalled by the discovery of the principal river of Australia. Here was an agreeable surprise, coming as it did in defiance of the prediction of Oxley, who was reckoned the highest authority of the period. Hume called this river after his father; but, forgetful of this fact, Captain Sturt, having hit it in its lower course, gave it the name of the Murray, by which it is now known through its whole length. The party who thus found themselves brought to a stand-still naturally looked upon the crossing of so large a river as a formidable undertaking, and some even insisted on regarding it as the limit of the expedition—perhaps homesickness also was beginning to prevail over their ardour for exploration. Hume was inflexible, as usual, threatening to throw one of the remonstrants into the river if he would not cross over of his own free will. The menace was effectual, and the heroic leader had the satisfaction of seeing the whole of the expedition on the other side of the Murray, having escaped without a hitch or accident. Soon after, a tributary, the Mitta Mitta, was reached, and crossed by means of a float constructed of wattles, and covered with a tarpaulin. Turning its course more to the westward, the expedition continued to advance towards the attainment of its object. Passing near the site of the present Beechworth, the Ovens and Goulburn Rivers were crossed without serious difficulty. In fact, the whole journey up to this point had been remarkably uneventful for an Australian tour of exploration. But for the leaders' quarrels and separations it might have sunk into a rather tame and monotonous affair. Now at length, however, a Titanic obstacle had to be encountered. Mount Disappointment (of which Mount Macedon is a continuation) stretched across the track, as if to defy further progress. For a while they nobly persevered in hewing their way through the dense, tangled, and apparently interminable brushwood, being animated by the assurance of Hume that the opposing barrier could be nothing else than the Dividing Range, which betokened the near termination of their labours. Unfortunately the life and soul of the expedition, now more than ever indispensable to its success, here met with a disabling accident from a stake. The way through the scrub had to be abandoned, and a more circuitous route followed. The most serious difficulty on the march was a boggy creek in the locality where the town of Kilmore now stands. Here again an attempt was made to throw up the undertaking and return home. Hume, feeling certain in his own mind that they could not have much further to go, entered into a compact with the discontents, engaging to turn back in the course of two or three days should the goal of the journey fail to come in view within that period. On the same day, the 13th December, the Dividing Range, in this part known as the Big Hill, was finally crossed, and all difficulties came to an end. Hume, having proceeded a short way in advance, and keeping an anxious look-out, observed an opening in the mountains and a falling of the land toward the south. This was a clear token heralding the approach to the close of their wanderings. Hume, alone as he was, gave way to an outburst of gladness, and awoke the echoes of the ranges with his lusty cheers. His men came speedily round him and shared his joy. Their fatigues and disappointments were henceforth things to be remembered, but no longer felt. The same evening they encamped on the splendid Iramoo Downs, having the ramparts of the range at their backs, and in three days more saw the long-desired billows of the ocean rolling at their feet. Having reached the close of the journey, they formed the last encampment within twelve miles of the present town of Geelong, after travelling, since their start from Lake George, not less than 670 miles.

CHAPTER V.

ALLAN CUNNINGHAM'S EXPLORATIONS.

Few visitors to the Sydney Botanic Gardens can fail to notice a memorial obelisk standing on a shady islet in the lower grounds. This monument, as the inscription declares, was erected in memory of Allan Cunningham, an eminent botanist, and for some time curator of these Gardens. But beyond the scanty information here given, very little is now generally known of the life and work of this worthy man. Restrained by that modesty which is so often a concomitant of real genius, he shrank from publicity during his own brief and busy lifetime; and posterity, ever too forgetful of the obligations of the past, have allowed his achievements to lapse into unmerited oblivion. This is flagrant ingratitude which should be brought to an end by a generous endeavour to resuscitate a heroic and patriotic memory.

Allan Cunningham was born at Wimbledon, England, on the 13th of July, 1791, and was of Scotch extraction on the father's side. Being designated for the bar he entered in due time upon the legal profession, but soon abandoned it as uncongenial to his tastes and habits. The study of botany proved an irresistible fascination to young Allan, who soon became a proficient in this science. Having been introduced to

Sir Joseph Banks, he obtained, through his influence, an appointment as King's Botanist for Australia, with the view of furnishing the Royal Gardens at Kew with a collection of new plants from the southern hemisphere. He sailed, accordingly, for his destination; and, after spending a short time in Brazil, landed in New South Wales, probably in December, 1816. As noticed in a preceding chapter he was associated with Oxley in his expeditions to the Lachlan and Macquarie rivers, and it was during these wanderings that the young botanist conceived a passion for exploration which did not leave him till the day of his death. This tour being ended, Cunningham returned to Parramatta, where he fixed his home, so far as he had one, during his life in Australia.

In the close of 1817, the *Mermaid*, under the command of Captain, afterwards Admiral, King, was preparing to leave Port Jackson on a voyage of discovery on the western coast of Australia. Cunningham, to his intense satisfaction, received a letter from Sir Joseph Banks, directing him to join this expedition, in the interest of botanical science. Sailing through Bass' Strait the *Mermaid* came to anchor in King George's Sound and other harbours, which proved to be well suited for the botanist's purpose, and yielded 300 species of new plants. With this spoil he came home fully satisfied. His next essay in this field was an excursion to Illawarra, which was always a favourite district with him. But this ramble was only an interlude. In 1819 he again joined Captain King in an expedition to the Macquarie Harbour, on the western coast of Van Diemen's Land (Tasmania), where also he collected many valuable specimens for the Kew Gardens. Soon after he was again associated with the same navigator on another voyage to the north-western coast. Still two more expeditions to the same coast were undertaken and successfully carried out within the next two years. The results in every case were highly successful, and the boundaries of science gained further extension from these enterprises.

Having spent four years on these voyages with King, Cunningham became inoculated with the spirit of adventure, and thirsted for an exploit on his own account. The feat he proposed to himself was to open a practical route from Bathurst to the Liverpool Plains. This splendid district, as already narrated, had been discovered by Oxley three years previously; but he had entered it from the western side—so to speak, by the back door—on his journey from the marshes of the Macquarie. The discovery had, consequently, been useless, and the Liverpool Plains were as yet known only by name. Sir Thomas Brisbane, the Governor of the day, entered heartily into Cunningham's scheme, having clearly understood the importance of the object in view. Orders for an equipment were issued to the full extent of the explorer's requirements. All things being ready by the 31st of March, 1823, the party, consisting of the leader, with five men, and five pack-horses, carrying provisions for ten weeks, left Parramatta for Bathurst, which was reached on the 5th of April, and then the northward journey commenced. After many weary stages, during which the patience of the men and the strength of the horses were severely tried, they reached the Warrambungle Mountains, which form the southern boundary of the Liverpool Plains; but the difficulty in finding a passage through this barrier appeared to be insuperable. The first fortnight was spent to no purpose in attempting to discover an opening on the south-eastern side. Almost in despair, the party retraced their steps and fell back on a former encampment on the Goulburn River, the principal tributary of the Hunter. Provisions were now getting short, and the allowance had to be reduced; but, in spite of all these dispiriting circumstances, Cunningham still resolved to prosecute his enterprise by making another struggle to find an entrance from a different point. Turning now to the north-west, and searching along the front of the range, he succeeded at last, on the 5th of June, in discovering a gap which afforded a good passage into the Liverpool Plains. To this entrance he gave the name of Pandora's Pass, believing it would become the chief if not the only means of communication between the settlers at Bathurst and the Hunter River and the occupants of the plains. The following memorandum was buried in a valley immediately below the pass:—

"After a very laborious and harassing journey from

Bathurst, a party, consisting of five persons, under the direction of Allan Cunningham, H.M. Botanist (making the sixth individual), having failed of finding a route to the Liverpool Plains, whilst tracing the south base of the barrier mountains (before us, north), so far as 50 miles to the eastward of this spot, at length, upon prosecuting their research under this great mountain belt, north by west from this tree, to the very extensive levels connected with the above-mentioned plains, of which the southernmost of the chain is distant about 11 or 12 miles N.N.W. from this valley, and to which a line of trees has been carefully marked, thus opening an unlimited, unbounded, and seemingly well-watered country N.N.W. to call forth the exertions of the industrious agriculturist and grazier, for whose benefit the present labours of the party have been extended. . . . Buried for the information of the first farmers who may venture to advance so far to the northward as this vale; of whom it is requested that this document may not be destroyed, but carried to the settlement at Bathurst, after opening the bottle."

This memorandum was found a few years ago, and the explorer's directions carried out. The object of the expedition being now accomplished, the party returned on the homeward track, and Allan Cunningham reached Parramatta on the 21st of July, 1823.

In the next important enterprise he is found associated with Oxley, exploring the country around Moreton Bay. They surveyed the Brisbane River, pushing up the stream as far as was practicable in their boat. It turned out to have but a short course, and they were disappointed in their expectation of being carried for some distance into the interior. Yet this labour had the negative value of satisfying the public that the Brisbane was not one of the great rivers of Australia. The King's Botanist again found rich spoil for the Royal Gardens at Kew.

During the winter months of 1825, being again bent on travel, Cunningham started for a northern tour. Leaving Parramatta, he crossed the Hawkesbury and proceeded towards Wollombi, one of the tributaries of the Hunter River. Still pushing ahead he reached Mount Danger, then Pandora's Pass, and entered upon the Liverpool Plains. These he now found to be a region of swamps and marshes as the consequence of a rainy season. Having crossed this district as best he could, the ardent traveller pressed on through Camden Valley and reached Dunlop's Head, at no great distance from the River Darling, which, with a little presentiment, he might soon have discovered and anticipated Captain Sturt. But as the country was now beginning to dip perceptibly, being in many places covered with water, which had accumulated during recent wet weather, he deemed prudence the better part of valour, and abandoned a hopeless enterprise. He was again in his own home by the 17th of June, having travelled in all about 700 miles.

After a short season of rest, during which New

Zealand was visited, this untiring scientist returned to the colony and offered himself for further exploration with renewed zest and zeal. The time was opportune, for the Governor had been anxiously looking about for a suitable leader to conduct an expedition to the distant north. Cunningham's offer was therefore eagerly accepted, and ample provision made for his requirements. All things being ready, the start was made on the 30th of April, 1827, with six picked men and eleven heavily-laden horsemen. The route skirted the western flank of the Liverpool Plains, and by the 11th of May the party entered upon ground hitherto untrodden by civilized man. A fine valley now opened to view, and was named the Stoddart, in remembrance of an old friend of the explorer's. The Namoi River was next forded, and by the 25th the hilly country on the west had sunk into the plain. The scene that now lay before them will be best described in the words of the leader of the expedition. "A level open interior of vast expanse, bounded on the north and north-west by a distant horizon, broke suddenly on our view. At north-west, more particularly, it was evident to all of us that the country had a decided dip, and in that bearing the line of sight extended over a great extent of densely wooded or brushed land, the monotonous aspect of which was here and there relieved by a brown patch of plain; of these some were so remote as to appear a mere speck on the *ocean* of land before us, on which the eye sought anxiously for a rising smoke as indicative of the presence of the wandering aborigines, but in vain; for, excepting in the immediate neighbourhood of a river of the larger magnitude, these vast solitudes may be fairly said to be almost entirely without inhabitants. We had now all the high grounds on our right, or to the east of us, and before us, to the north, a level wooded country." These plains which ran out towards the western interior, having turned out to be drier than was expected, the line of route was now directed more to the north and north-west, with the result of discovering and crossing the Dumaresq River, within a few days. The course next lay for some time through a poor and inhospitable country in which the jaded horses fared badly enough. By the 5th of June, this sterile belt was left behind, and now the eyes of the patient explorers rested on one of the finest regions they had ever beheld. For many a league north, east, and west the field of vision was filled with a panorama of boundless plains, rolling downs, and azure mountain ranges. This magnificent territory, rivalling a principality in size, was clad with luxuriant vegetation and generally well watered. The name Darling Downs was subsequently bestowed on this fine country in honour of Governor Darling, and it now forms one of the most valued possessions in the colony of Queensland. The average elevation of this table-land Cunningham found to be about 1,800 feet above sea-level. Had this worthy man performed no other public service during his lifetime, the discovery of the Darling Downs would have given him a strong claim on the gratitude of posterity.

Having now sufficiently realized the aim of the northern expedition, Allan Cunningham ceased to push farther in that direction, and made eastward for the coast. Here also was made an important discovery on a smaller scale in the unexpected appearance of a fertile valley, with a river of greater size than a mountain stream. To both the valley and the river he gave the name of Logan, in compliment to the commander of the penal settlement at Brisbane. The expedition tarried for some time in this lovely vale, where both men and beasts of burden enjoyed much-needed repose. Cunningham himself, who scarcely understood what rest meant, botanized as usual, and examined the physical configuration of the country. On a fine morning he scaled one of the impending peaks, from the summit of which he obtained a comprehensive view of the situation and its surroundings. To the south-east, at the distance of 60 or 70 miles, the towering cone of Mount Warning, the sailor's beacon, rose in impressive grandeur; while towards the north-east the environs of Moreton Bay were plainly visible. This latter revelation made it obvious that the proper route to the Darling Downs would be from Moreton Bay, by the Brisbane River, and through the Main Range. Hence it became a matter of the first importance to find a passage through the mountains, if within the bounds of possibility. An effort was accordingly made, and an opening, as he believed, discovered, but its complete verification had to be deferred till another opportunity. The homeward journey was resumed on the 16th of June. On the 30th, the Dumaresq River was crossed 50 miles above the outward bound track of the expedition. In ten days more a large river was reached, and is now well-known under the native name Gwydir. They next came upon a wooded tract, reached by a descent of 1,200 feet, a sore task for the weary horses. On the 19th the party were again on the Liverpool Plains, and a few days' more travelling brought them to their welcome homes. They had journeyed over 800 miles, and been absent thirteen weeks. One noteworthy incident connected with the tour was the paucity of native inhabitants met with in any of the districts. Only five times, from first to last, had the black-fellows put in an appearance, and even then the explorers had seen nothing but the colour of their skin.

Cunningham's health now began to give way, and he longed to return to old England, to end his days in the land of his birth; but, before doing so, he planned and executed another exploring excursion to Moreton Bay. His principal object was to obtain certain evidence of the existence and practicability of the pass, which he believed to have been already discovered. After much rough work he had the good fortune to set this question at rest and point out a passage into the Darling Downs, as he had formerly done into the Liverpool Plains. This pass still retains the name of Cunningham's Gap. The following succinct but sufficient notice is found in the explorer's own notes:—" This pass, or door of entrance from the sea-coast to a beautiful pastoral country of undefined extent, seen from this point, was this day (25th August, 1828) visited by Allan Cunningham and a convict servant, and the practicability of a high road being constructed through it at some future day was most fully ascertained. The pass is in latitude 23° 3′ S., and longitude 152° 26′ E., and distant 54 statute miles from Brisbane Town." Four years later he was able to carry out his purpose of returning to England; but his heart was in Australia all the while, and he became impatient to get back to its sunny skies and balmy air. On being offered the situation of Colonial Botanist he accepted the appointment, and returned to the land of so many of his labours; but his new office was not what he expected. Besides keeping the Botanic Gardens, which would, alone, have been a most congenial occupation, he was required to act as landscape gardener for the upper classes and take charge of one hundred convicts, forty of whom were lodged in the barracks within the Gardens, and for whose good behaviour the curator was alone responsible. In addition to all this drudgery he was compelled to grow vegetables for the Government officials. Such servitude was breaking his heart, and it can surprise no one to find him throwing up the appointment in disgust. This undignified treatment of a man of shining merits is tartly alluded to in the *Sydney Mail* of the 29th January, 1838 :—

"THE BOTANICAL, ALIAS THE KITCHEN GARDEN.— We have had frequently to call the attention of the colonists to the fact that a kitchen garden, under the pretence of a botanic garden, is supported in Sydney at an expense of from £800 to £1,000 a year. We scarcely ever walk through this garden without seeing some servant with a basket, carrying off vegetables or fruit for Mrs. This or Mrs. That, the wife of some official. Can't these people go to market and purchase their supplies as independent persons do, instead of poaching on what is really public property. Seriously we do say that such an impudent job should be done away with. It is, in fact, so barefaced that Mr. Cunningham would no longer consent to remain a mere cultivator of official turnips and cabbages, and accordingly he has resigned the management of the Botanic Garden in disgust."

This valuable life was now fast hastening to its close. Twenty-five years of incessant labour, often performed under the most trying circumstances, broke down a constitution never particularly robust, and feeling this to be the case, Allan Cunningham retired from public view into his own hired house—but only to die. At the early age of 48 years, perceiving the hand of death to be upon him, he calmly resigned himself to the will of his Maker, and died as becomes a christian. He expired on the 27th of June, 1839. Admiral King, who had stood his firm friend during the quarter of a century of Cunningham's active life, refers to his own bereavement in these touching words:—" Alas, poor Allan! He was a rare specimen, quite a genus of himself; an enthusiast in Australian geography; devoted to his own science, botany; a warm friend, and an honest man; and, to crown all, when the time came, he resigned himself into the arms of his Saviour without a murmur."

CHAPTER VI.

CAPTAIN STURT'S THREE EXPEDITIONS.

THE next hero that steps to the front is Charles Sturt, captain of the 39th regiment, which was stationed at Sydney in the early days of our history. He stands, beyond all question, in the first rank of Australian explorers. His single compeer, Sir Thomas Mitchell, was more fortunate in discovery, but it may be doubted whether he excelled Captain Sturt in real capability for this work. The future historian will probably decide the rival claims by bracketing the two names as holding a joint first in Australian exploration. Naturally brave, resolute, and patient in labour, Sturt was, moreover, a man of varied culture and extensive scientific acquirements. As an officer in the army he had been accustomed to command, and at no time did he experience any difficulty in managing the several exploring parties under his charge, although they were mostly drawn from the ordinary convict element at Port Jackson. This influence over others may have been due to natural tact even more than to acquired habit, but in either case it proved a valuable qualification, and served him in good stead with the native population as well as with his own men. His heroism often brought him into situations of extreme peril, being sometimes environed with savages well armed and out of all proportion to the number of his own men; but his adroitness never failed to extricate himself and party from the most imminent danger. Scarcely any of our explorers opened up so much of the interior, or so frequently came into contact with savage tribes, and yet his humane disposition preserved him all through his career from shedding the blood of a single individual of that unhappy race which others, with less excuse, have not scrupled to shoot down like dogs. When stooping under the weight of years, with a constitution enfeebled by heroic exertions, and so afflicted with blindness as to be unable to finish his narrative without the aid of an amanuensis, the veteran explorer devoutly thanked God that, amid all his critical encounters and hair-breadth escapes, he had been saved from the necessity of shedding a drop of blood from the veins of the Australian aborigines.

I.

As early as the year 1818 the Macquarie River had been explored as far as practicable by John Oxley, the Surveyor-General. This indefatigable traveller had traced its course into the far interior till it seemed lost and appeared to terminate in a series of swamps, overgrown with dense reeds. All his efforts to proceed further westward proved unavailing, and he turned aside to other work, being under the impression that he had seen all that was visible of the Macquarie. Like some others of his time, Oxley had taken up with the idea of a mediterranean sea which was supposed to cover the interior of Australia; and such being his opinion, it was natural to fancy he had reached its margin in those swamps of seemingly indefinite extent into which the Macquarie poured its flood. During the next ten years Cunningham had pushed as far north as the Darling Downs, while Hume and Hovell had been equally successful in forcing their way south to Port Phillip; but out west no progress was made beyond the goal of Oxley's explorations. But ignorance of the interior hung like a cloud over the settlement, a vague feeling of mystery kept curiosity awake, and a general desire began to be expressed for fresh explorations in that direction. The times, too, which in other respects happened to be signally disastrous, appeared to be just as favourable for such an enterprise. A drought of several years' standing was then devastating the colony; but this misfortune, which brought ruin to the doors of so many settlers, seemed, strangely enough, to be a strong recommendation to start an exploring expedition. It had been Oxley's misfortune to examine the country during an exceptionally wet season, and it was conjectured that floods had laid under water the low-lying country on the further reaches of the Macquarie, and thus interposed a temporary obstruction to the westward advance of exploration. But now, after a drought of long standing, it was hoped that the swamps, if not dried up, would at least be so much reduced as to render the much-desired object more likely to be accomplished.

Governor Darling, accordingly, determined on

sending out another expedition. In the all-important question of a leader, he was singularly fortunate in selecting Captain Sturt. The latter took as his associates Mr. Hamilton Hume, who had already gained his own laurels in exploration, Staff-Surgeon M'Leod, two soldiers, and eight convicts. The instructions received from headquarters were, generally, to follow up the discoveries of Oxley, to endeavour to ascertain the "fate" of the Macquarie, and to put forth the utmost effort to penetrate westward to the furthest possible limit.

All the material requisites for the expedition were forwarded to Wellington Valley, which at that time was the outpost of civilization toward the west, and Sturt was instructed to form his depôt at Mount Harris, which had been Oxley's most advanced encampment ten years earlier. All preparations being made, the party left Sydney on the 10th of September, 1828, under the command of Captain Sturt, who only a week previously had followed the remains of Oxley to the grave. After a few days of uneventful travelling through the settled territory, Wellington Valley was reached, and, by the 10th of December, the explorers were encamped at Mount Harris, the *ne plus ultra* of their predecessors, and near the supposed termination of the Macquarie River. Although ten years had passed away, traces of the old camp were easily found. From the summit of the mountain a good prospect towards the interior was obtained, and a tolerably favourable impression left on the minds of

Sturt and Hume. The marshes were seen to be dried up in some places altogether, and in others very much contracted, and, as the bed of the river continued to be well defined, there did not appear to be much difficulty in pushing the limit of discovery considerably beyond the line at which it had stood for ten years past.

Following the course of the Macquarie for some miles westward, it was found to enter a swamp of considerable size. As the sluggish current was the only clue to lead them through this ambiguous tract of land and water, it was deemed indispensable to keep to the channel at all hazards as it meandered through the marshes. For this purpose Sturt here turned to account a good-sized boat which had, with a wise foresight, been provided among the travelling requisites. But their progress by water proved to be less expeditious than it had been on the land, for the channel wriggled like a snake, and the navigation was provokingly hindered by snags. Gradually the course of the river became better defined, but only to lose itself again in a labyrinth of creeks and marshes. Puzzled and bewildered, with no hope of further progress in the boat, Sturt and Hume resolved to make separate excursions to the right and left, each taking his own complement of followers. Many hardships had to be endured from heat and drought, while the results were not very considerable. Sturt rode over 200 miles of desert country and was much fatigued. The principal discoveries made about this time were Oxley's Table-land and New Year's Creek, mistaken by the explorers for a branch of the Macquarie, but which was in reality the Bogan River. Eventually both sections of the expedition reunited and bravely struck out for the interior, giving defiance to thirst and fatigue, and devoutly wishing for something to turn up. They had not far to go till this desire was realized. At a moment when they were not thinking of it, the foremost of the party found their progress stopped on the bank of one of the principal rivers in Australia. Its ample channel extended to seventy or eighty yards in breadth, and its bosom was covered with wild fowl of every wing. Almost perishing with thirst, both man and beast rushed down the shelving bank, and in a moment were gulping down the water of the welcome stream. Never did travellers meet with so "bitter" a disappointment. "I shall never forget," says Sturt, "the cry of amazement or the look of terror with which they cried out to inform me that the river was so salt as to be unfit to drink." The cup of relief was dashed from their lips, and they were left to the most gloomy reflections on the future supply of this element. They conjectured, not unnaturally, that this saline quality must be derived from near contact with the sea, and anxiously watched for the slightest indications of a rising or a falling tide, but to no purpose. The cause was afterwards traced to briny springs in the river's banks, which must have been a temporary occurrence, for the same inconvenience is not met with now. The discovery in all other respects was clearly perceived to be of the utmost value, and went far to annihilate the pet theory of an inland sea, which thus kept receding further and further from human ken. It was already evident that this noble river must play a principal part in the drainage of the western slope of the mountain ranges, and we now know that it forms the backbone of the river system of eastern Australia and the highway of intercolonial commerce. Sturt, therefore, paid Governor Darling no mean compliment in associating his name with this grand discovery and calling it the Darling River.

The expedition now followed the lead of the River Darling for about sixty-six miles. As the country continued to be inhospitable, the blacks troublesome, and the supply of water precarious, it was resolved to proceed no further in that direction. A return was accordingly made to the depôt at Mount Harris, which was reached partly by way of New Year's Creek, or the Bogan River, without any serious mishap being encountered.

Among the secondary instructions given to the expedition was a direction to push northwards, if baffled and driven back from the western interior. They had not failed in that quarter by any means, but as their work there was finished, and a good supply of provisions left, it was thought advisable to attempt a journey to the Castlereagh, which was simply known to exist. In this effort they were again successful. Having travelled by way of Morriset's Ponds, a sufficient supply of water was obtained to help them on to the Castlereagh, where, of course, it was expected to be abundant, seeing that Oxley had been able to cross it after some delay and with much difficulty. But this anticipation was doomed to disappointment. The bed of the river was found to be as dry as dust. The explorers, after a long search, hit upon only one small pool in the sand which yielded but a temporary supply. The Castlereagh was now traced towards its supposed junction with the Darling for the distance of 100 miles, 45 of which were destitute of water. But their perseverance was rewarded with a second view of the Darling, which was struck about 90 miles above the point where the original discovery had been made. The stream here swarmed with fish, but was still salt and unfit to drink. Having crossed over to the further side, a dash was made by a short excursion into the interior, which proved, like the other side, to be a parched wilderness. The state of the country as observed throughout this journey is thus summed up in Sturt's narrative :—" So long had the drought continued that the vegetable kingdom was almost annihilated, and minor vegetation had almost disappeared. In the creeks weeds had grown and withered and grown again, and young saplings were now rising in their beds nourished by the moisture that still remained; but the largest forest trees were drooping, and many were dead. The emus, with outstretched necks, gasping for breath, searched the channels of the river for water in vain; and the native dog, so thin that it could hardly walk, seemed to implore some friendly hand to despatch it. How the natives subsisted it was difficult to say, but there was no doubt of the scarcity of food amongst them." Surely this was no place to loiter in after the work was fairly accomplished. Contenting themselves with the substantial discoveries already made, the explorers resolved to return to the haunts of civilization. They soon found themselves in the lovely Wellington Valley, from which the expedition had been absent four months and a half. After another journey through the settled districts, each of the weary wanderers reached his home, no one having sustained any injury to life or limb during this long and hazardous enterprise.

II.

Captain Sturt enjoyed but a very limited repose after the fatigues of the Macquarie expedition. He had returned to Sydney about the beginning of May, 1829, and in September of the same year his undying enthusiasm was once more gratified with instructions from headquarters to get ready for a full exploration of the Murrumbidgee. The Macquarie and the Lachlan, terminating their respective courses in miserable swamps, or being believed to do so, had proved delusive guides to the interior of the continent. But the colonists were resolved to know the heart of Australia at all hazards. It was still believed that some river must lead thither, all previous disappointments notwithstanding. The Murrumbidgee alone remained as an untried experiment, and the little that was yet known of this river gave hope of a successful result. It had been first seen by two military officers, Currie and Ovens, on their discovery of the Monaro country in 1823, and in the year following it was crossed with difficulty by Hume and Hovell on their journey to Port Phillip. Here, at last, was a stream something like those of other countries, rising in the Alpine mountain-land, and flowing with a strong and rapid current in that direction to which the eyes of explorers were being so anxiously turned. It was determined, therefore, to equip another expedition, under the command of Captain Sturt, to explore its unknown course, for the purpose of ascertaining whether it emptied itself into an inland sea or found its way to the southern or to the eastern coast. The party, under Sturt's leadership, consisted of Mr. George Macleay, son of the Colonial Treasurer, Mr. Frazer, botanist, and six others. Among other requisites a whaleboat was provided, which eventually proved of the utmost service to the purpose in view.

The expedition left Sydney, in full force and high spirits, on the 3rd November, 1829. Goulburn Plains were reached by the 15th, and on the 25th the Murrumbidgee was struck, not far from Jugiong. The appearance of the stream was quite up to Sturt's expectations, but the rugged country on its banks delayed the passage of the drays, and their progress was not very rapid. In a little time they reached the junction of the Dumot (Tumut) River, which considerably increased the volume of the Murrumbidgee, and this addition was accepted as a good omen. In their course along the river, sometimes on one side and sometimes on the other, occasional plains were traversed, extending from 400 to 700 acres in extent, and wholly devoid of timber. Lower down the river one of much larger size was reached, and here the explorers were not sorry to make a short break in the journey. The natives called this plain Pondebadgery. Its size was three and a half by two miles, the soil being rich and the scenery exquisite. On one side was the bend of the river, here 80 yards wide, and abounding in fish, one of which was found to weigh 40 pounds. Hamilton Plains were next discovered, and named after a favourite staff-surgeon. The expedition, it was believed, had now come within 25 miles of the most southern point attained by Oxley. This notable explorer, having reached the swamps of the Lachlan, and being thus driven to his wits' end, resolved to strike southward and make for the coast, but want of water determined him to return to the Lachlan, after weeks of toilsome travel; whereas, had he only pushed on another 25 miles, the Murrumbidgee would have been discovered, and a new era opened in Australian exploration. Sturt attempted to connect the surveys of Oxley's expedition with his own, but was not successful. As travelling continued to be slow and difficult, it was resolved to launch the boat and build a skiff to convey the provisions. This was accordingly done, some of the party being at the same time sent back to Goulburn with the drays. Seven days having been consumed in these preparations, the remainder of the party boldly committed themselves to the stream. Sturt had a strong presentiment that the Murrumbidgee would join some other river, and hoped to find it navigable for his boat during the remainder of its course. On the following day a serious mishap occurred. The skiff was sunk by a snag, and the provisions, after being much damaged, had to be recovered by diving. The enterprise was a hazardous one at the best. What with rapids at one time and snags at another, their lives on several occasions were in real jeopardy. But the longest lane has its turning, and this tortuous channel also had an end. On the seventh day after taking to the boat the bed of the river became strangely contracted, and the current so powerful that, in place of rowing, all their strength was needed to steady the boat, which was borne along with the swiftness of an arrow, and in another moment shot forth impetuously into the broad reach of the finest river in Australia. "It is impossible for me," says Sturt, " to describe the effect of so instantaneous a change of circumstances upon us. The boats were allowed to drift along at pleasure, and such was the force with which we had been shot out of the Murrumbidgee that we were carried nearly to the bank opposite its embouchure whilst we continued to gaze in silent astonishment on the capacious channel we had entered, and when we looked for that by which we had been led into it we could hardly believe that the insignificant gap that presented itself to us was indeed the termination of the beautiful stream whose course we had thus successfully followed. I can only compare the relief we experienced to that which the seaman feels on weathering the rock upon which he expected that his vessel would have struck, to the calm which succeeds moments of feverish anxiety, when the dread of danger is succeeded by the certainty of escape." This was indeed a noble river. Its width was 350 feet, its depth not less than 12, and its current was running at the rate of two and a half knots an hour. The discoverers believed they had now obtained ample reward for all their toils and trials. This was the same river which had been discovered and crossed by Hume and Hovell where the town of Albury now stands, but between that point, where it had been first seen by civilized man, and the part now visited by Sturt, it had received so many tributaries as to make it a much larger and, in a sense, another river. Sturt called it the Murray, after the Imperial Colonial Secretary, but the original discoverer had named its upper course the Hume in memory of his father. For a time these names were confined to the respective parts of the river; and Dr. Lang censured Count Strzelecki for departing from this usage in his published work. General practice has now deserted the Doctor and followed the Count.

The number and persistent hostility of the aborigines

formed a serious obstacle to the progress of this expedition. It was computed that no fewer than 4,000 were met with on the Murray. They were a low type even for Australian savages, and did not give evidence of a single redeeming quality. Addicted to every vice, living in the deepest sink of bestiality, with bodies in many cases rotting with disgusting diseases, they presented a loathsome spectacle, and were avoided whenever possible. Even when not disposed to be openly hostile, their presence at the camp was a terrible nuisance, and they were generally persuaded to leave, or hunted away. Sometimes they would rally their forces, and then prove not only troublesome but really dangerous. Like all savages they were adepts in deceit, and could wait their opportunity when a purpose had to be served. By dint of numbers and strategy together, they nearly succeeded on one occasion in annihilating the expedition. So long as the river maintained its usual width the boat was tolerably safe in the middle of the channel, for the spears of the savages were nearly harmless when they reached the centre of the stream, but their progress was rapidly approaching a spit which stretched far into the channel, and this position was seen to be occupied by blacks numbering more than fifty to one of Sturt's party. The situation was awfully critical, and in a few minutes more appeared to be positively desperate, for the boat grounded in shoalwater, and the explorers were at the mercy of the savages. Happily at this juncture some other natives, who had previously been friendly to the white men, arrived on the scene, and, through a somewhat barbarous style of intercession, prevailed with their sable fraternity in the interest of Sturt, and the murderous attack was immediately abandoned.

Travel through an unknown country is usually a series of surprises, and it was no ordinary one that was now in store for the explorers. The spit which had threatened to be so disastrous proved to be an embankment silted up by the entrance of another large river into the Murray. Sturt had already been looking out for the junction of the Darling, which he had discovered on the previous expedition; and the question now to be determined was whether this could be the embouchure of the same river. He had struck the Darling at two points only a few months before, and at both places its water had been found too salt to drink; here, however, it was quite fresh; but in all other respects appearances were in favour of this river, and the Darling Sturt maintained it to be. For years after his decision was disputed, and even ridiculed by an authority of no less weight than Sir Thomas Mitchell. Subsequent exploration finally settled the question in Sturt's favour. The river was and could have been no other but the Darling, and thus another important problem of Australian geography was satisfactorily solved.

Day after day the boat, with its adventurous crew, glided down the united stream of the Murray and the Darling. Sometimes they passed over wide and long reaches, stretching out for many miles, but occasionally, too, much difficulty was experienced in clearing the rapids. For a considerable part of the course the banks were high and steep, but usually picturesque. The country, so far as could be judged from a passing boat, was mostly of the poorest quality, offering scarcely a patch likely to reward the labour of the farmer. In one respect Sturt was the most unfortunate of the explorers. From first to last he hardly ever had the good luck to hit upon a large tract of fine country, the Alexandrina district excepted. His mission seemed to be the discovery of deserts, and of these he made known more than enough to give Australia a bad name. Such being Sturt's ill-fortune, it is not surprising to find him indulging in gloomy views regarding the great interior; but even in these forebodings he fell short of Oxley, who was quite a Cassandra in his way. In the introduction to his narrative the Captain tries to account for the predominance of poor land in this outlying region of the world, and is inclined to attribute it to the want of decaying vegetable matter, as the trees seldom shed their leaves, and the little that is supplied from this or other sources being usually destroyed by bush fires. But Australia is not the desert land which Sturt imagined, or even portrayed, as will be seen further on. Its richest lands were yet locked up, and this same explorer was unconsciously preparing the key by which they were to be opened to private enterprise and the public benefit. Between the entrance of the

Darling and what is now known as the Great Bend an important tributary was observed to fall in from either side. The one from the north Sturt called the Rufus, in honour of Mr. George Macleay, the second on the expedition. Probably the reader fails to perceive the point of the compliment. It lies just here: Mr. Macleay possessed a splendid head of red hair, and *rufus* being the Latin for red, down it went for the name of the river. The Captain, notwithstanding his sombre tinge, must have had a quiet vein of humour in his composition. The other tributary was called the Lindsay, after a gentleman of that name who was then Acting-Governor of the colony. On gaining the lower reaches of the Murray it was observed to widen rapidly, and at the 35° 15′ of S. latitude expanded into a magnificent lake 60 miles long and 50 in width, which was named Alexandrina, in honour of the young princess, who soon after became Queen Victoria. When the far end of the lake had been reached, persistent but unavailing attempts were made to get the boat to sea. Before leaving Sydney it had been arranged to send a small vessel to St. Vincent Gulf to wait for the expedition, that being the most likely quarter for it to turn up if its course should be directed towards the southern coast. The appointed rendezvous was not far off, and the explorers had every reason to strive to reach it; but it was to no purpose that they wearied themselves in the effort. The narrow and tortuous channel which connected Lake Alexandrina with Encounter Bay was impracticable even for a boat. It was, therefore, necessary to return by the way they had come. This was an awfully serious matter. They had now been 32 days in the boat, during which one-half of the provisions had been consumed. If the depôt on the Murrumbidgee was to be reached on the remaining moiety, it could only be by rowing up the river in the same period of time they had taken to glide down the current. This appeared to be scarcely possible, but all their strength was put forth, and they displayed such pluck and perseverance as shed enduring lustre on the heroism of Australian exploration. " Our journeys," writes Sturt, " were short, and the head we made against the stream but trifling. The men had lost the proper and muscular jerk with which they once made the waters foam and the oars bend. Their whole bodies swung with an awkward and laboured motion. Their arms appeared to be nerveless, and their faces became haggard, their persons emaciated, their spirits wholly sank—nature was so completely overcome that, from mere exhaustion, they frequently fell asleep during their painful and almost unceasing exertions. I became captious, and found fault where there was no occasion, and lost the equilibrium of my temper in contemplating the condition of my companions. No murmur, however, escaped them, nor did any complaint reach me that was intended to indicate that they had done all they could do. I frequently heard them in their tent, when they thought I had dropped asleep, complaining of severe pains and of great exhaustion. 'I must tell the Captain to-morrow,' some of them would say, 'that I can pull no more!' To-morrow came, and they pulled on, as if reluctant to yield to circumstances. Macnamee at last lost his senses. We first observed this from his incoherent conversation, but eventually from his manner. He related the most extraordinary tales, and fidgetted about eternally in the boat." In such a plight did they reach the depôt on the Murrumbidgee. Altogether 88 days were spent in the boat, and the distance travelled could not have been less than 4,000 miles. The rest of the journey was performed by easy stages, the party arriving in Sydney on the 25th of May, after an absence of almost seven months.

III.

The discovery of a rich territory on Lake Alexandrina, was made in 1830, and before another decade had passed away the settlement of South Australia was established in this promising region. By a singular fatality, Sturt, as an explorer, had the infelicity of stumbling continually upon deserts, or on tracts only a shade better; but the termination of the Murray, which he had navigated so courageously, brought him to the borders of an ample area of the richest land in Australia. In these circumstances it was natural for him to evince a special fondness for the locality which had been the most fortunate, as it was also the latest, of his discoveries. The retired explorer accordingly settled down with his family in this chosen haunt, with the intention of making his permanent home in the young colony of South Australia. He received a civil appointment as Surveyor-General, which enabled him to live in comparative quiet and comfort, and he was highly respected for his great services to Australia in general. After so many years of retirement, probably no one expected to hear anything further of Charles Sturt as an explorer. It could not, therefore, fail to produce a feeling of surprise when it became known that after fourteen years' repose he had sought and obtained from Lord Stanley the necessary requisites for another expedition into the interior. He had again become fired with his old ambition, and was now covetous of the honour of being the first European to plant his foot on the centre of Australia. All things being in readiness for this heroic undertaking, Sturt left Adelaide on the 15th of August, 1844, with a party of fourteen men, amply provisioned. He chose the route of the Darling and Murray rivers, which he proposed to follow till the outskirts of civilization were reached. The Murray was struck at "Murrundi," the residence at that time of another noted explorer, Mr. E. J. Eyre, who had recently accomplished his adventurous journey round the Great Australian Bight, and the river valley was thereafter traversed as far as the junction of the Williorara, a locality better known now under the name of the Laidley Ponds. This place was becoming known to overlanders, and it was hoped it might prove a suitable site for the first depôt; but this expectation was hardly justified by personal inspection, and it became evident that the expedition must proceed at once into the interior. Sturt accordingly gathered his party around him, and, having engaged in appropriate devotional exercises, in which he committed himself and his men to the watchful care of Almighty God, launched bravely forth into the perils of the wilderness. Some distance ahead a mountain chain was visible, to which the name of Stanley, or Barrier Range, was afterwards given. The march was at first directed towards these heights, in the hope that a river might be discovered on the opposite fall which would lead into the interior. Here again expectation was doomed to disappointment, and the expedition was forced to proceed along the range, where water alone was to be found. Gradually the mountains sank into the plains to the northward, and it was resolved to strike out for the centre from this point, taking the risk of obtaining a sufficient supply of water at tolerable intervals. The country traversed in this direction proved to be cheerless and sterile in the extreme, and the journey was tedious and trying to a corresponding degree. Nevertheless, the party pressed forward, doing their best to deserve success. But it was to no purpose. The country became still more inhospitable, and water utterly failed. It was evident that the object of the expedition could not be reached by this route, and Sturt, wearied in body and chafed in spirit, was compelled to retreat to the mountains on his outward track. This was his first repulse from the centre of Australia.

A return was made to the depôt, which had fortunately been established not far from the range, in a lovely oasis in the desert. No reader of the narrative of the expedition can soon forget the strange incidents of this depôt in the Rocky Glen, which unexpectedly became the prison-house of the whole party for six months. The supply of water here was good and abundant, though not inexhaustible; and this advantage was of supreme importance, as a drought of unparalleled severity was fast closing in upon the expedition. Being wearied and worn out by the toilsome journey to the northward, Sturt resolved to give his men a brief breathing time in this favoured spot; and when this temporary repose was ended he found, to his consternation, that his retreat was cut off, while it was equally impossible to advance. Here is his own description of the heat and misery they had to undergo:—"The tubes of the thermometer burst, the bullocks pawed the ground to get a cooler footing, the men's shoes were scorched as if by fire, their finger nails were brittle as glass; the lead dropped from the pencil, the ink dried in the pen, as Sturt wrote up his daily journal; the drays almost fell to pieces, the screws loosened in their boxes, the horn handles of the instruments and their combs split, the wool on the sheep and their own hair ceased to grow." Many persistent efforts were made on every side to find a way of escape; but all to no purpose, for the drought had closed them in as effectually as a besieging army. There was no help for it but to make the best of their misfortune until rain came to the rescue. Fortunately they had sufficient feed and plenty of water for their live stock, and for such mercies they were truly thankful. As the summer advanced it was found necessary to seek a partial refuge from the scorching rays of the sun in an underground chamber, which had been constructed for this purpose. The imprisonment had, at the same time, a few negative advantages. For one thing, the completeness of their isolation formed a sufficient safeguard against the assaults of the barbarous tribes of the interior; for the same calamity which prevented the one party from getting away equally prohibited the other from approaching this oasis in the desert. During the six months' detention only one blackfellow had been able to put in an appearance, and not till reduced to the last extremity of hunger and thirst. The poor emaciated creature was prevailed upon to remain for the present; but, having free access to the explorers' mutton, he grew tolerably fat in the course of a fortnight, when, with the usual gratitude of the barbarian, he turned his back upon his benefactors and took the way that pleased him best. The accounts of the interior which Sturt received from this and other aborigines he had previously encountered were disheartening in the extreme, and it was impossible to abstain from gloomy forebodings during this period of enforced incarceration.

But whether they were to have any more travelling or not was becoming more and more a matter of bare probability. The herbage of the valley had become reduced to mere dust, and the water had diminished so ominously as to make it apparent that, unless rain fell within a month, the party would certainly find their graves in the Rocky Glen, as one of them had already done. But the future had better things in store, and did not longer withhold them. In one of those sudden changes so characteristic of the Australian climate the sky assumed its curtain of clouds and burst in a storm of rain, which deluged the valley. The roar of the rushing water, Sturt avers, was the sweetest music that ever fell upon his ear. That welcome thunderstorm was the key which opened the door of the prison and gave liberty to the captives.

This happy release was followed by a period of successful travelling—not, indeed, void of difficulty, but yet without much of stirring incident. Another depôt was formed, which is well known under the name of the Park. Having enjoyed a short breathing time here, the expedition again proceeded eastward, and touched on the northern extremity of Lake Torrens. A survey of this part having been made, in accordance with special instructions, they returned to the Park Depôt, which was reached just twelve months after Sturt had left Adelaide. As time was thus rapidly passing away, he now resolved to put forth all his strength in a bold effort to reach the summit of his ambition and place his foot on the centre of Australia. Wishing to have as little encumbrance as possible, he divided his party, and, having picked three of the best men, started for the goal of his weary journeys, leaving the remainder in the depôt. Day after day this forlorn hope toiled on. Plain succeeded plain over a dreary expanse of interminable country, redeemed only by a series of parallel watercourses, which afforded a sufficient supply of that indispensable element. One important creek was crossed, but had to be abandoned, as it headed in a wrong direction. Happily, a sufficient compensation was found in the discovery of another creek, which they called the Eyre, after the adventurous explorer; and this godsend in the wilderness they were able to follow for a long distance. It was after they were compelled to leave it that they entered upon the stern realities of travel in the untrodden interior. The country now assumed an aspect so sterile and forbidding as to place it out of comparison with anything which Sturt, the discoverer of deserts, had previously witnessed. For a space of 20 miles nothing was found but a series of sand-ridges succeeding one another with the monotonous regularity of the waves of the sea. The fatigue which had to be endured in crossing this inhospitable tract was indescribable. It greatly weakened the strength of the party, and it was only the hope of soon meeting a change of country which lured them on. Nor was this expectation doomed to disappointment, for a change they met with at a moment's notice. All of a sudden the jaded explorers found a stony desert springing up beneath their feet and stretching away as far as the eye could reach, while it included within its ghastly embrace more than half the horizon. The suddenness of the appearance of this spectre of desolation struck them mute with surprise and horror. One of Sturt's attendants was the first to break the silence, which he did by raising his hands and exclaiming—"Good heavens! did ever man see such country?" Probably he never did. It is worse even than the African Sahara. It is beyond the power of words to describe it as it stands in its lone and dread reality. Sturt's Stony Desert is one unbroken expanse of desolation, a wilderness of red ferruginous sandstone, undergoing perpetual disintegration, constituting a natural ruin on a gigantic scale, without a single redeeming feature. Barrenness has marked this region for her own, and will ever hold it as a special possession. No life can subsist within its borders; the foot of the savage is not upon its wastes, and the whole region is still and silent as the grave. Such is the dark picture as drawn by the explorer himself. Happily a better acquaintance has led to a more favourable opinion; though the land of spinifex, it produces other vegetation of nutritive and even fattening properties. The Stony Desert proper consists of many patches, but probably none will be found to be very extensive. The stout hearts of the explorers quailed but for a moment. Be the consequence what it might, they determined to go forward, and the first night found them encamped in the desert without a drop of water. Their only hope of safety consisted in expeditious travel out of this scene of desolation. It was found to extend 50 miles, and when the party reached the other side, they were in a condition which can be more easily conceived than described. Here again they entered upon a similar belt of sand-ridges such as they had found flanking the Stony Desert on the other side. These, unhappily, were succeeded by another region of sand, utterly destitute of water. Their sufferings, which had formerly been great, were now intolerable. It became apparent that further progress was impracticable, and it was just a question whether retreat was possible—certainly it could not remain so much longer with such heat and drought as were then prevailing. The necessity of retreat was thus forced upon them, but it was a very painful one. They had now travelled more than 400 miles from the depôt (and such travelling!) and could they only have advanced another 150 miles they would have pitched their camp in the centre of Australia, the darling object of so many heroic sacrifices. Their reluctance to yield to this last dictate of necessity was extreme. A member of the expedition has pictured Sturt as he sat on one of the sand dunes with his face buried in his hands for a whole hour, while the struggle was going on in his own mind. It was not in nature, indeed, to yield without a mighty conflict. But inexorable necessity had to be obeyed notwithstanding, and thus valuable lives were saved. This was his second repulse from the centre of Australia. Nothing is more admirable in the character of Sturt than his magnanimity under adversity. However keenly he may have felt his disappointment, his mind retained its accustomed tranquillity, and during the retreat he went on laying down the bearings of his route for the guidance of others who might follow and obtain the palm he had been compelled to resign. He reached the depôt, where he had left the remainder of his party, on the 2nd October, 1845, having been absent seven weeks and travelled more than 800 miles.

After a short period of rest and refreshment this chivalrous explorer, who amid all his heavy misfortunes was certainly *tenax propositi,* to the surprise and regret of his party conceived the design of making one more attempt to reach the centre of Australia. He now determined on trying the line of the creek he had formerly discovered, and now called after Strzelecki, in the hope of its giving him sufficient northing to bring him within a practicable distance of the object for which the expedition had been sent. Strzelecki's Creek was found to answer his purpose so long as it lasted, and at its termination led to the discovery of another of much greater importance. To this new river Sturt gave the name of Cooper's Creek, after a distinguished South Australian judge. Unfortunately it flowed nearly east and west, and, therefore, had to be abandoned in the prosecution of a northern route. Leaving the plains which extended for some distance from the banks of Cooper's Creek, Sturt again encountered the ominous sand-ridges of which he had had sufficient experience on the former journey, and these being traversed, his hard fate again landed him on the edge of the Stony Desert. His destiny seemed ever mocking him with deserts, but this was the last he ever discovered. Having swept the unvarying horizon long and patiently with his telescope, and finding no break in the terrible monotony, he turned back for the third and last time from the effort to accomplish the dream of his life. After so many magnanimous sacrifices, he finally and for ever waived the palm of reaching the centre of the continent, which, sixteen years later, was won by a member of the same expedition, Mr. J. M'Douall Stuart, whose march to the coveted spot reads in comparison like a holiday excursion. The party now fell back upon Cooper's Creek, which was traced upwards for a considerable distance. It is a remarkable circumstance that Sir Thomas Mitchell was exploring its upper waters about the same time. But nothing could be more diverse than the two descriptions of the same stream. Mitchell's is quite *couleur de rose*, and Sturt's has probably been tinged with the effect of his own misfortunes. While the one gave it the name of Cooper's Creek, as already noticed, the other called it the Victoria, after the Queen. This was most unfortunate, as there is another Victoria River on the west coast. However, both designations are now generally superseded by the native name of Barcoo.

It is unnecessary to enter into details respecting the homeward expedition. The outward track was followed as closely as possible to Laidley Ponds, and thence to Adelaide. The water was rapidly drying up, and the retreat had to be conducted like the forced marches of an army. The men were nearly all ill, more or less, and some of them, being unable to walk, had to be carried long distances. Latterly, the leader of the expedition seems to have been the chief sufferer. Long exposure to the glaring reflection of the sun on the sandy wastes had ruined his eyesight, and not long afterwards he became permanently blind. Even now his constitution was completely shattered, and he had to be laid on a bed of leaves and conveyed from the interior in a cart, from which sufferings he never fully recovered. Such was Charles Sturt, after fifteen months' wanderings in the deserts of our country; and henceforth this heroic and much-enduring man disappeared from the stage of Australian history, of which he had been long a distinguished ornament. He retired on a pension of £600 from the South Australian Legislature, and died at Cheltenham in 1869.

CHAPTER VII.

EYRE'S ADVENTUROUS JOURNEY ALONG THE GREAT AUSTRALIAN BIGHT.

EDWARD JOHN EYRE, the son of a Yorkshire clergyman, was born in the year 1815. A youthful passion for the heroic led him to chose the military profession; but, having failed to obtain a commission, he turned his attention to the colonies, and came to Sydney in 1833, with the slender capital of £400. Part of this sum was spent in obtaining colonial experience, in which he graduated so high as to become the leader in a new Australian enterprise. The newly founded settlements of Port Phillip (subsequently Victoria) and South Australia had created a great demand for stock, all of which had hitherto been carried by sea, and, on reaching their destination, were sold at famine prices. Young Eyre conceived the practicability of an overland route, and proceeded to prove it to a demonstration. In the first of these journeys he took 1,000 sheep and 600 head of cattle from the Monaro district, in New South Wales, to Adelaide, in South Australia, by way of the Murray River, and reaped a handsome pecuniary reward in the sale of the stock. Smaller men followed in the wake of this born adventurer, making overlanding the most paying game in Australia, till a glut was produced in the southern markets. Success having followed Eyre in the new path his enterprise had struck out, he was soon in possession of sufficient funds to begin squatting on his own account. He purchased the station "Murrundi," on the Lower Murray, where he resided for several years, acting also as magistrate and protector of the aborigines. Occasionally, too, he varied the monotony of bush life by feats of exploration into the unknown territory, thus keeping alive the spirit of adventure, and unconsciously qualifying himself for the romantic enterprise which will transmit his name to distant posterity.

Up to the year 1840 Western Australia remained completely isolated from the other colonies, and could be approached only by sea. But as that country was now being extensively occupied, it was of great importance also to the settlers in the south to find an overland route from Adelaide, and it was believed the time had come when a successful effort could be made. The obstacles which barred the way were enormous, and for that epoch insuperable; but so little were they suspected by the South Australians that the proposed journey was regarded as a pleasure excursion, and it was considered advisable to lighten the expense of the expedition by sending over a quantity of stock with the pioneer explorers! The one man who could correct this public delusion was Mr. Eyre, for he knew enough of the outlying country to feel safe in predicting the failure of the proposed undertaking. By both speech and pen he laboured to oppose the misguided enthusiasm, and succeeded in preventing a certain waste of treasure and a very probable sacrifice of human life. But it was far from his desire to see so much ardour for exploration run to waste, and now that the colony was in high feather for discovery, Eyre made a successful effort to divert it into what he considered a more profitable channel. Very little was yet known of the country to the north. Why not strike out in this direction now, and make a bold attempt to reach the centre of Australia from the city of Adelaide? One argument alone was sufficient, and with it Eyre prevailed. He offered to be the leader of the expedition, providing one-third of its expense from his own pocket. Nothing remained now but to get on with the preparations.

On the 20th of June, 1840, a well-provisioned party consisting of eight persons, with Eyre in command, supported by two other Europeans, Scott and Baxter, left Adelaide under favourable auspices, and in high hopes of exploring a large portion of the interior if more cherished results should prove unattainable; but, as the event proved, only to meet with crushing disappointment. Lake Torrens was as yet very imperfectly known, and Eyre, misled by refraction, conceived it to be an immense sheet of water in the shape of a horse-shoe, within the bend of which he supposed the expedition was being entrapped. The curve, in reality, was described by a chain of mud lakes partly covered with water, and partly encrusted with salt. Passages are now found, at intervals, between these mud lagoons, but Eyre had not the good luck to hit on one of them. Aroused by the energy of despair, he next determined to round this impenetrable barrier, and struck out to the eastward, for an isolated peak which he called Mount Hopeless. The name corresponded to the reality, for the outlook from its summit revealed nothing but a barren and burning desert, which forced the expedition to fall back by a western route to the southern coast.

Headquarters now remained for some time at Streaky Bay, on the eastern shoulder of the Great Australian Bight. Taking a subdivision of the party, he again and again endeavoured to round the head of the Bight in the hope of finding better country, which would open a favourable route towards the interior. Here, too, his expectations were baffled in this latter respect, and even Eyre had to abandon his pet project in utter despair. But he was of too dauntless a temperament to brook the idea of returning to Adelaide without accomplishing something worthy of remembrance. His next move was competent only to a madman or a hero. It was a serious attempt to lead an expedition from the encampment on Fowler's Bay to King George's Sound, along the Great Australian Bight, a journey of more than 1,500 miles over the worst country under the sun. He proposed to proceed with his present party unbroken, if Governor Gawler would allow the government cutter to advance to Cape Arid, a sort of half-way station, and there await the expedition, with a supply of provisions. The Governor refused the use of the vessel in connection with so romantic a proposal, except for the purpose of bringing the entire party back to Adelaide, and so putting an end to what he must be excused for regarding as a mad freak. But Eyre was a man born to lead, not to be led, and determined to stick to his purpose, with help or without it. Yet, being conscious of the extreme peril that lay on the very face of the undertaking, he resolved to risk the sacrifice of no European's life but his own, and made preparations to send home Scott and Baxter in the cutter. Baxter, an old and faithful servant, who had been overseer on Eyre's station, persisted in clinging to his master, whether for life or death. And, alas! it was for the latter. The party, as thus reduced, consisted of only two white men and three black boys, one being an old favourite named Wylie. A few horses and sheep, together with a limited supply of provisions, made up the sum total of the expedition.

Never before was an enterprise of such overwhelming difficulty engaged in by reasonable men. This section of the southern coast was yet scarcely known. The navigators Nuyts and Flinders had cruised over its waters, gazing with mysterious awe on its weather-beaten cliffs, rising to the precipitous height of 400 or even 600 feet above the water. At intervals along the base the waves had undermined this Titanic sea-wall, causing it to fall in many a yawning breach, the *debris* of which completely obstructed the passage between the rocks and the sea in the few places where such a convenience might have been previously possible. The crown of these cliffs had not yet been trodden by the white man's foot, and the reports of the sparse aborigines were enough to freeze the ardour of the most adventurous in the heroic age of Australian exploration. On this border-land of earth and sea contending winds had deposited the dust particles borne on their wings, and rolled them together in heaps, to be met with at long and dreary intervals. These sand-hills, resting on a limestone formation, retained at their base a small supply of water, to be reached only by painstaking, and often painful, digging. For the greater part of the way no other water was to be found on this barren and inhospitable region of parched-up Australia.

From Cape Adieu, where leave had been taken of the cutter and its passengers, to the first stage at the head of the Bight, the difficulties were manageable— for this part of the route had been traversed and supplies hidden for future use—but, this over, they had to be faced in all their appalling magnitude. The sand-hills were found to be so far apart that it was impossible to bring the stock from the one to the other without intermediate supply. When the sheep, and sometimes the horses, could travel no further, one or two of the parties had to be left in charge while others pushed forward in search of water, and then returned with what supply they could bring, when the animals were driven on to the station. The discouragements were infinite and the labour superhuman. Eyre alone was equal to the strain, and he owed it more to his indomitable spirit than to his natural strength. It was a sore trial to perceive even Baxter to be giving way and wishing to return; but as this seemed to threaten certain death, he kept to his resolution, and persevered against all hope of a successful issue, so desperate had the aspect of affairs now become. The few sheep having dwindled away with ominous rapidity, it had become necessary to kill several of the horses and eat them, although they furnished little but skin and bone. Matters having come to extremities, the baggage had to be reduced to the smallest proportions, and most of the valuables were thrown away in the wilderness to lighten the burden of carriage. Their sufferings from want of water now became indescribable. Man and beast were compelled to travel three or four days without getting a mouthful. With only one exception, none had been found but in the sand-hills for the distance of 800 miles, and how hard it was to reach it there has already been described. Even the dew on the sparse patches of grass was put in requisition, as may be learned from the following extract from the journal of the expedition:—"Leaving the overseer to search for the horses, which had strayed, I took a sponge and went to try to collect some of the dew which was hanging in spangles on the grass and shrubs. Brushing these with the sponge, I squeezed it, when saturated, into a quart-pot, which in an hour's time I filled with water. The native boys were occupied in the same way, and, by using a handful of fine grass instead of a sponge, they collected about a quart among them. Having taken the water to the camp and made it into tea, we divided it amongst the party, and never was a meal more truly relished, although we ate the last morsel of bread we had with us, and none knew when we might again enjoy either a drink of water or a mouthful of bread. We had now demonstrated the practicability of collecting water from the dew. I had often heard from the natives that they were in the habit of practising this plan, but had never before actually witnessed its adoption."

But the climax was yet to come. To privations and difficulties the crime of treachery and murder was now to be added. Two of the blacks proved unfaithful, and shot the overseer, Baxter, in cold blood, apparently for the purpose of deserting with as much of the provisions as they could lay hands on, perhaps after the murder of the leader himself. The words in which Eyre describes the anguish of his situation exceed the highest efforts of tragedy, and show how fact may become stranger than fiction. "The night was cold, and the wind blowing hard from the southwest, whilst scud and nimbus were passing very rapidly by the moon. The horses fed tolerably well, but rambled a good deal, threading in and out among the many belts of scrub which intersected the grassy openings, until I scarcely knew exactly where our camp was, the fires having apparently expired some time ago. It was now half-past ten, and I headed the horses back in the direction in which I thought the camp lay, that I might be ready to call the overseer to relieve me at eleven. Whilst thus engaged and looking steadfastly around among the scrub to see if I could anywhere detect the embers of our fires, I was startled by a sudden flash, followed by the report of a gun, not a quarter of a mile away from me. Imagining that the overseer had mistaken the hour of the night, and not being able to find me or the horses had taken that method to attract my attention, I immediately called out, but no answer was returned. I got alarmed, and, leaving the horses, hurried up towards the camp as rapidly as I could. About a hundred yards from it I met the King George's Sound native (Wylie) running towards me, and in great haste and alarm, crying out, 'Oh, Massa! oh, Massa, come here!' but could gain no information from him as to what had occurred. Upon reaching the encampment, which I did in about five minutes after the shot was fired, I was horror-struck to find my poor overseer lying on the ground weltering in his blood, and in the last agonies of death. Glancing hastily around the camp, I found it deserted by the two younger native boys, whilst the scattered fragments of our baggage, which I left carefully piled under the oilskin, lay thrown about in wild disorder, and at once revealed the cause of the harrowing scene before me. Upon raising the body of my faithful but ill-fated follower, I found that he was beyond all human aid; he had been shot through the left breast with a ball; the last convulsions of death were upon him, and he expired almost immediately after our arrival. The frightful, the appalling truth now burst upon me that I was alone in the desert. He who had faithfully served me for many years, who had followed my fortunes in adversity and prosperity, who had accompanied me in all my wanderings, and whose attachment to me had been his sole inducement to remain with me in this last and, to him, alas! fatal journey, was now no more. For an instant, I was almost tempted to wish that it had been my fate instead of his. The horrors of my situation glared upon me in such startling reality as for an instant almost to paralyze the mind. At the dead hour of night, in the wildest and most inhospitable wastes of Australia, with the fierce wind raging in unison with the scene of violence before me, I was left with a single native, whose fidelity I could not rely upon, and who for aught I knew might be in league with the other two, who were perhaps even now lurking about with the view of taking away my life as they had done that of the overseer. Three days had passed away since we left the last water, and it was very doubtful when we might find any more. Six hundred miles of country had to be traversed before I could hope to obtain the slightest aid or assistance of any kind, whilst I knew not that a single drop of water or an ounce of flour had been left by these murderers from a stock that had previously been so small. Though years have now passed away since the enactment of this tragedy, the dreadful horrors of that time and scene are recalled before me with frightful vividness, and make me shudder when I think of them. A lifetime was crowded into those few short hours, and death alone may blot out the impression they produced."

To give decent burial to the body of a friend whom death only could separate would have been a melancholy satisfaction, but even this slight tribute of affection was denied by the situation. No grave could be dug, for sheet-rock, stretching far and wide, formed the adamantine pavement of this horrible place. Wrapt in a blanket for its winding-sheet, the corpse was left in this lonely wilderness, where it lay undisturbed till it was stumbled on quite recently by the district mailman. On a calmer view of the position, Eyre discovered that the ruffians had left him only forty pounds of flour, a little tea and sugar, and four gallons of water. Such was the provision for two men against a journey of 600 miles! Nothing, however, could be gained by delay in this awful scene, and every consideration counselled an immediate departure—most of all, the knowledge that the two murderers were skulking in the neighbourhood with the probable design of taking Eyre's life. A start was made without further loss of time. Another horse was killed for food, but the animal having been poor and sickly, its flesh did not agree with them, and ill health supervened. When thus brought face to face with the last extremity, a sudden vision of deliverance nearly overwhelmed them with joy. Coming unexpectedly on an opening in the Bight, first a boat and then a ship at anchor rushed upon the view. A closer acquaintance proved the apparition to be a French whaling-vessel, under the command of Captain Rossiter, whose name is fittingly perpetuated in the same little bay. The unlooked-for visitors were hospitably entertained and lodged for twelve days in the ship, till they were sufficiently recruited for the remainder of the journey. With renewed strength, and a fresh supply of provisions, the march through the desert was once more resumed, for the indomitable explorer would not even yet abandon the project. Though hardship had now lost its sting, more difficulties had yet to be encountered than might have been expected, but they were of a different kind from the preceding. Water became only too plentiful, for a wet season had set in, and the travellers had often to wade rather than to walk. But the end of this terrible journey drew on apace. To their unspeakable joy the mountains on the further side of King George's Sound began to loom in the distance, and Wylie, who was a native of that district, now for the first time showed some confidence in his leader, whom he never expected to bring him back to his home. The welcome sight, in truth, inspired both the black and the white man with fresh life; for they had to make only one more effort, and, this over, their weary feet found rest in the hospitable settlement of Albany. The heroic endurance displayed during this journey stands without a parallel in history, but it led to nothing but a barren triumph over stupendous difficulties. Had Eyre kept further inland he would have found a better route and opened up a more profitable country. This discovery had to wait for another and more fortunate explorer. The present expedition, by hugging the shore, travelled over a tract of country that was seen to be utterly useless for the wants of civilization. So patent was this fact to Mr. Eyre himself that he justified the publication of his narrative by the strange argument that no one had traversed this wilderness before and he was perfectly sure none would ever do it again.

Henceforward Edward John Eyre was known to fame—but not to fortune. Being subsequently appointed Governor of Jamaica, he fell heir to an upheaval of disorder, which culminated in open rebellion. This insurrection Eyre put down with an iron hand. Some accused him of needless severity, while others justified his conduct as an act of imperative necessity. The hero-worshipper, the late Thomas Carlyle, defended him bravely, and was seconded by many sympathizers of less note, who came to the rescue with pen and purse. This perilous journey of former years was justly pleaded in Mr. Eyre's favour, but his friends weakened their case by confounding the Great Australian Bight with the

Gulf of Carpentaria! Though exonerated by a commission of inquiry, the Governor was recalled, and for four years thereafter harassed by a bitter prosecution, which he probably found harder to endure than his terrible journey on the Great Australian Bight.

CHAPTER VIII.

SIR THOMAS MITCHELL'S FOUR EXPEDITIONS.

THIS eminent explorer was a native of Scotland, having been born at Craigend, Stirlingshire, in 1792. He chose the army for his profession, and served under Wellington, in the Peninsular war, from 1808 till its close. His career appears to have been a most creditable one. He had a hand in laying out the famous Torres Vedras lines, which gave a fatal check to the ambition of Napoleon. Mitchell left the service with the rank of Major, receiving also a medal and five clasps. Having emigrated to New South Wales, he was appointed Surveyor-General, an office which had fallen vacant by the death of Mr. John Oxley. Being an active and adventurous man, he threw himself, heart and soul, into the cause of exploration. Mitchell was the most successful of all the explorers, and had the good fortune to open up the magnificent territory which now forms the colony of Victoria. He was the leader of four great expeditions, which shall now be briefly related in the order of their occurrence.

I.

Among the notabilities of the old convict days there are not many who will be longer remembered than

George Clarke, better known, in his own time, as "George the Barber." This runaway convict having taken to bushranging and cattle-stealing as naturally as the duck makes for the water, had also shown himself an adept in the arts which elude the detective. Passing beyond the bounds of settlement, which had now extended 300 miles to the north of Sydney, he fixed his headquarters and erected a stockyard for stolen cattle on the further side of the Liverpool Plains. Here he abjured the last vestige of civilization and associated himself with the aborigines, having become a conformist in the first degree. He doffed every article of clothing, blackened his skin, and even scarified his flesh, in order to appear a naked savage pure and simple. But the compliment does not seem to have been reciprocated. He was successful, indeed, in gaining the hearts of two black gins, who followed him and his fortunes as far as fate would permit; but the sable brotherhood did not take kindly to the intruder. Hearing he was wanted by the police to answer for his cattle-stealing propensities, they lent a hand to the progress of civilization, and delivered up this spurious brother, who was forthwith lodged in Bathurst gaol. Of all the men in the world this runaway convict, who had enjoyed the sweets of liberty, both in the savage and the civilized life, would be the last to brook the restraints of confinement, and it is no surprise to find him casting about for the means of deliverance. The most feasible way of accomplishing his object undoubtedly lay in the plan which his native cunning led him to adopt. Popular excitement was then at fever heat on the exploration of the unknown territory. Sturt had recently returned from an expedition in which he had opened up more than 2,000 miles of country on the lower Murrumbidgee and Murray rivers, and had, consequently, given a great impulse to the exploring enterprise. Now was the time for "George the Barber" to tell his secret from Bathurst gaol. Having passed beyond a range of mountains to the northward of the Liverpool Plains, so his story ran, he had discovered a magnificent river which the natives called the "Kindur." It traversed a splendid country, was itself navigable throughout, and having followed its course on two different occasions, it led him through the heart of Australia to the north coast, without ever turning to the south. Men readily believe what they wish to be true, and such a river as here described was the very thing wanted in order to open up a waterway to Carpentaria. The story accordingly commanded general attention, and most people believed it contained a sufficient degree of verisimilitude to warrant the expense of a special exploring expedition to put it to the proof.

Major Mitchell was now in the place where he would feel the impulse for exploration with all its force, and so fell in most heartily with the popular excitement. Putting the most favourable construction upon the "Barber's" story, and believing that it contained, at least, a substratum of truth, he expressed his readiness to go in search of the "Kindur," provided the Acting-Governor, Sir Patrick Lindsay, would supply the necessary outfit. This request was readily granted, and Major Mitchell left Sydney on the 24th November, 1831, to run a wild-goose chase or make a great discovery. It was not necessary to organize the expedition before starting, as the country was now settled so far to the north, and final arrangements were accordingly postponed till a nearer approach was made to the unknown land. The early part of the journey was pretty much in the style of a pleasure excursion. The would-be explorer of the "Kindur" passed northward to Parramatta, where he was shown, as a great novelty, the first olive-tree planted in the colony. The Hawkesbury was crossed at Wiseman's Ferry, and in due course the Wollombi, a tributary of the Hunter, was reached. Soon after he proceeded to make up his party, which, when completed, consisted of two gentlemen volunteers, named White and Finch, and fifteen convicts, all of whom, the leader avers, were ready to face fire and water in the hope of regaining that liberty which they had forfeited by transgressing the laws of their country. The expedition having been thus organized and supplied with every requisite, moved northward, passing near Muswellbrook, and crossing the Hunter without meeting with anything particularly worthy of notice, until they came upon the burning hill of Wingen, which attracted their attention as a remarkable curiosity. It is not a volcano, but a mountain of coal or shale, on fire underneath, which sends forth volumes of smoke through the rents in its surface. On the 5th of December the ascent of the Liverpool Range was gained and a commanding view of the plains obtained. This fine tract of country had been discovered by Oxley, explored by Cunningham, and was now found to be largely occupied by pioneer squatters. The Peel River was struck at Wallamoul, about two miles above the spot where Oxley had first crossed it, and here was found the last station, owned by a squatter of the name of Brown, and containing 1,600 head of cattle. The route of the expedition was now directed towards the lower course of the river, where it becomes known under the native name of the Namoi. The euphonious "Namoi" was music to the ear of Mitchell, for the bushranger had spoken of a river of this name, and was the first to make it known under this designation. The Major was gratified to find this slight confirmation of the story that had brought him so far from home, and hastened to make it known to the authorities in Sydney, that "George the Barber" might have the benefit; and a real benefit it was, for it saved him from the gallows. Having failed to obtain his liberty when his information was acted on, this noted criminal, in his desperation, succeeded in sawing the irons off his feet, and in this way made good his escape from incarceration. But the law has long arms, and the "Barber," being again clutched within their iron grasp, was condemned to suffer the last penalty, from which doom he was saved by the timely arrival of Mitchell's letter.

The *terra incognita* now was entered upon, and the first object that drew the attention of the explorers was the old stockyard of the bushranger, which, doubtless, was too near a neighbour of Brown's cattle station. About two miles distant the Pic of Tangulda rose to a conspicuous elevation. This was one of the landmarks of the prisoner's tale. The "Kindur" was to be reached by proceeding north-east, over a range of mountains which were visible from this position. Mitchell directed his march accordingly; but, after several days of distressing travel, found the mountains to be impracticable, and was compelled to return to his former camp. Now, for the first time, grave doubts began to fill his mind regarding the truth of the convict's story. No other course being open, he determined on launching a canvas boat and making an effort to sail down the Namoi, to see what fortune had in store for him. The attempt was scarcely well made when it had to be abandoned, on account of snags and shoals in the stream; but the change of position was sufficient to make it apparent that the mountain-chain which could not be crossed might now be turned. This achievement was next successfully accomplished, and Mitchell at length found himself on their northern flanks. These mountains bore the native name of "Nundawar," and, in respect of their outward appearance, had been described sufficiently well by the bushranger. But now came the crucial

test of his truth or falsehood. According to the same
story the "Kindur" was the first river to be reached
beyond these mountains, and, one way or other, the
question could not now have long to wait for an answer.
A river of some kind was the very thing wanted by
the explorers, for they had passed through a rugged
and waterless country. Were they now, at last, to
drop upon the "Kindur?" Such a discovery would
have been doubly welcome, for it would have relieved
them from present distress, and proved the goal of a
journey which, it was hoped, would place the laurel
crown on the brow of the Major and sound the trumpet
of freedom to his fifteen convict attendants. The 9th
of January arrived, and this day was destined to feast
the eyes of the weary travellers with the sudden
appearance of a noble river, broader and deeper than
the Namoi, and one of which Australia might well be
proud. Was this the "Kindur" at last? Not for a
moment. It flowed in the wrong direction, and lost
much of its volume in its downward course; and
Mitchell soon satisfied himself that it was nothing else
than one of the many tributaries of the Darling. In
fact, it had not the merit of an original discovery.
This was the Gwydir, which had been crossed long
ago by Allan Cunningham. Mitchell turned from it
in disgust and made for the north, in the hope of
hitting upon some discovery really worthy of the
expedition. He was rewarded, in so far that he
discovered an important river, called the Karaula by
the natives, but now better known as the Macintyre.

Further exploration proved this stream to be one of the head-waters of the Darling, and, therefore, useless for the purpose of one who was seeking a water-channel to the Gulf of Carpentaria.

Mitchell's only hope of retrieving himself now lay in crossing the Darling, and making an inroad upon the interior; but the feasibility of this course was suspended on a doubtful contingency. Fearing his provisions would not hold out so long as would be necessary, he had, before leaving the Peel River, sent Finch back to the Hunter district for fresh supplies, and the future of the expedition depended on this forlorn hope. Finch returned about the time expected, but only to bring a tale of disaster instead of a supply of provisions. All had gone well till they had got beyond the Liverpool Plains, when water began to fail them. Finch had gone on to search the country in advance, and on returning found his party murdered and the camp sacked. This was a crowning calamity. Mitchell, of course, now saw that it would be impossible to proceed further, and it was even very doubtful whether they could return in safety. A wet season was setting in, and 200 miles of flooded country lay between them and their homes. Their return, accordingly, was conducted after the manner of a retreating army, and the similitude was all the more striking because they were harassed by hostile tribes of aborigines. But the settled districts were soon reached, and there was no further difficulty in making Port Jackson. It was, indeed, a disappointment to the authorities, as it had been to Mitchell, to find they had been duped by "George the Barber." Yet the expedition had opened up a vast extent of pastoral country, and on the whole was fairly successful as an exploring enterprise.

II.

Major Mitchell, full of enterprise, was again in the field of discovery in 1835. His failure in the affair of the "Kindur" had not discouraged him, and the experience incidentally gained was an excellent preparation for the more arduous work of the future. Public attention had again turned from the north to the westward of the colony, and another attempt was to be made to lift the veil which still shrouded so much of the interior. At the request of the British Government, Mitchell willingly undertook the conduct of an expedition to the Bogan and the Darling, in order to set at rest some geographical problems which were still attached to the course of these rivers.

More than any of the other explorers, Mitchell believed in large and liberally equipped expeditions, here probably erring by excess, and he resolved that the present should not be deficient in either respect. The party, all told, consisted of twenty-four persons—Major Mitchell as leader, Richard Cunningham, brother to the more celebrated Allan Cunningham, botanist and explorer, a young surveyor of the name of Larmer, and twenty-one convict servants, nine of whom had been connected with the "Kindur" search. The material resources consisted of two boats, several drays, a good contingent of horses, bullocks, and sheep, together with an ample supply of provisions. The start was made from Parramatta on the 9th of March; but the work of exploration proper did not commence till they reached Buree, a frontier station near Mount Canobolas, about 170 miles from Sydney.

Having taken his observations from the summit of this mountain, Mitchell fixed his direction on the bearing of 60° west of north, judging he would thus find a practicable route, and strike the Bogan somewhere in its upper course. The result answered his expectation. On the 13th of April he crossed the Goobang, a tributary of the Lachlan, and in two days more the Bogan was reached. Here a most lamentable event occurred, which cast its dark shadow over the whole of their future wanderings. Richard Cunningham, the botanist of the expedition, had been too much in the practice of leaving the party for the "pursuit of flora," and now failed to find his way back to the camp. For a long time no trace of the missing man could be found; but after a most diligent search tracks both of himself and of his horse were observed. These were followed for 70 miles, but to no purpose; distressing suspicions also began to arise, pointing to foul play on the part of the natives. But nothing definite could be arrived at, and after a fortnight's fruitless searching and tracking, the expedition was sorrowfully compelled to hold on its course. Subsequently it was decisively ascertained that Cunningham, ready to perish of hunger and thirst, had sought refuge with the blacks, by four of whom he was savagely murdered in his sleep. A full investigation was made by Captain Zouch, who had been despatched from Sydney on this business. He succeeded in discovering the dead man's bones, which were decently interred, and a suitable monument was erected on the scene of this diabolical murder. Three of the perpetrators of the crime were also arrested; but, through the remissness of the constable in charge, two of them managed to escape.

The explorers still kept the line of the Bogan, moving off and on to its banks according as the want of water, or the desire to cut off an observed elbow, more particularly directed their course. By the 20th of May the expedition had arrived at the Pink Hills, where the best grazing land was met with since the commencement of the journey. From this point Oxley's Table-land, a well-known landmark with former explorers, was plainly visible. On the 25th they were gratified by the discovery of the junction of the Bogan and the Darling rivers. The former of these, though only now brought into prominent notice, had been known to exist for many years past. It was first discovered by Hamilton Hume in connection with Sturt's expedition to the Macquarie, and was then called New Year's Creek. Much later its upper course had been traced by a Mr. Dixon for 67 miles, and the exploration of its whole length was thus completed by

Major Mitchell in 1835. The Bogan was found to head from the Hervey Range, and this explorer had the good fortune to discover its termination in the Darling River after a sinuous course of 250 miles. At best it is only a third or fourth-class river; but, as it traverses a tolerably good grazing country, its basin has become fully occupied for squatting purposes.

The junction of these two rivers now became an important landmark for the remainder of the journey, and the place has ever since played a conspicuous part in the opening up and settlement of the back country. The position consists of an elevated plateau overlooking a reach of the river a mile and a half in length, with a hill situated near a sharp turn at the lower end of the reach. Having now travelled 500 miles from Sydney, the whole party were in need of rest, and Mitchell wisely resolved on fixing a permanent depôt here. Intending to leave some of his men while engaged in the exploration of the lower course of the river, he considered it an act of prudence to enclose the depôt with a stockade, as he was not yet sufficiently acquainted with the natives of the Darling to trust them with any degree of confidence. A stockade was accordingly constructed of rough logs, and to this, his first attempt at bush fortification, he gave the name of Fort Bourke, in compliment to the Governor of the colony. Such was the beginning of Bourke, the now famous centre of our back country settlement, and the present terminus of the Great Western Railway of New South Wales.

Two boats, as already noticed, had been brought all the way from Sydney as part of the furniture of the expedition, and the time seemed to have arrived for their being turned to account. Being found to be in perfect order they were forthwith christened the *Discovery* and the *Resolution*, and launched on the feeble current of the Darling. But hope was excited to no purpose. The stream was too low and the channel too much impeded to permit of navigation even with the smallest craft, and the undertaking was no sooner initiated than it had to be abandoned. The former plan of the expedition had again to be adopted, and the progress on the Darling was very similar to what it had been on the Bogan. The country traversed was found to be inferior as a whole, only moderately valuable for pastoral purposes, and nowhere adapted for agriculture to any considerable extent. The incidents in this part of the march were neither numerous nor striking. The usual privations arising from want of water were hardly known, as the explorers were never far from the banks of a running stream which takes rank among the foremost in Australia. The saltness of the Darling, which proved such an inconvenience to Sturt, was found by Mitchell to exist in a much less degree, which shows that it must have arisen in part from temporary causes.

If Mitchell's narrative is not so rich in thrilling incidents as a sensational reader could have wished, it is especially valuable as a record of the manners and customs of the aborigines of those districts, as they appeared to the eye of this intelligent and observant traveller. Sometimes the description is so life-like that we are almost cheated into the belief of a visible reality, and it is impossible to be indifferent to the exhibition, although the whole race has now well-nigh passed away. The account is very generally the reverse of Captain Sturt's, notwithstanding that both of these eminent explorers must have had in view substantially the same tribes. The judicious reader will scarcely be disposed to agree unreservedly with the Captain when he depicts them as the "most miserable wretches" under the sun; neither will he care to subscribe to the unqualified language of the Major, who describes them as "happy" savages. Truth seldom lies in extremes, and it is to the utmost extreme that these authorities have gone, each in his own way, as determined largely, perhaps, by his idiosyncrasies. But the ethnologist, in particular, will be thankful for the literary photograph of these vanishing tribes which has been preserved in the pages of this journal. The general reader, too, will gladly observe some curious incidents of aboriginal life in the interior of Australia. Mitchell specially notices their adroitness in procuring the wild honey of the bush. With great tact they first attached a piece of light down to the bee, which, on being released, would be sure to make straight for its nest. To discover this secret, the blackfellow engaged in hot pursuit; and, as his eye must be constantly on the tiny insect, there would, of course, be frequent tripping, and many an awkward fall on mother earth, but the excitement was too great to permit of anything short of a serious accident being noticed. Another characteristic of the untutored savages was their unwillingness to recognize the right of a white man to hold property—it was all *meum* and no *tuum* with them. For a while Mitchell tried to satisfy them with liberal gifts, but giving only increased the craving for more; and, what was worse, this liberality on the part of the strangers began to be construed as an indication of fear, and then the demands were more impudently pressed than ever, which caused these gifts, very properly, to cease altogether. And now their thieving propensities broke out beyond all bounds. Mitchell, like Apollo when Mercury filched his bow, hardly knew whether to smile at the adroitness of the thief or wax indignant at the loss of his property. The cunning, craft, and success of these barbarians went almost beyond credence. Not only their hands were busy, but their very feet and toes picked up the strangers' tools as they walked over them. This latter practice was considered a real accomplishment, and these savages seemed to have a genuine contempt for the clumsy white-fellows who could not use their "feet fingers." Barring this troublesome propensity, the native tribes did not cause much inconvenience to the expedition until it got as far down the Darling as the Menindie quarter, where a serious embroglio occurred, which occasioned the shedding of aboriginal blood, and compelled the explorers to desist from the further prosecution of their journey. For this untoward event, however, Mitchell was not to blame, and he regretted he had to deal with convicts who were so difficult to control. The local tribes having thus become exasperated, a somewhat hasty retreat had to be made to the central depôt at Bourke, after 300 miles of the Darling had been traversed, and little doubt being left as to the remainder of the course till the junction with the Murray.

III.

The exploration and settlement of Victoria are quite recent events in the history of Australia. Important discoveries had been made on the seaboard by Bass and Flinders in the close of the last and the beginning of the present century; but they had no effect in attracting population. Hume and Hovell made an overland journey from Lake George to Port Phillip in 1824, and brought to light an enormous extent of fine territory near the southern coast; yet the country remained unvisited by civilization for another ten or twelve years. The original settlers came from Tasmania, and were crowded out of the old rather than attracted to the new home. The first arrival seems to have been Edward Henty, who effected a settlement at Portland Bay in 1834. Next year John Batman, a native of Parramatta, who had latterly resided in Tasmania, crossed Bass' Strait, and fixed his headquarters on Indented Head. He bargained with the natives for 600,000 acres of the best land in exchange for a few blankets, knives, and such-like commodities. He was followed in three months' time by another of the name of Fawkner, who, leaving "King John" in undisputed possession of Indented Head, pitched his tent on the site of the present city of Melbourne.

So much and nothing more was accomplished in the settlement of the premier part of Australia, when Major Mitchell crossed the Murray, and astonished the world by a series of splendid discoveries in what is now the famous colony of Victoria. The surprise was the more telling on this account, that the revelations resulted from a mere accident, and were aside from the proper object of the expedition. The explorations of Mitchell during the preceding year, which had so largely supplemented the earlier discoveries of Sturt on the Darling, very naturally excited public interest, and created a desire for another expedition. The River Darling was now pretty well known, with the exception of about 200 miles from Menindie to the junction with the Murray; but this latter river was not yet explored higher up than its confluence with the Murrumbidgee. These two objects being now to be prosecuted, instructions were given to Major Mitchell to organize another expedition; and into this project, it is needless to say, the gallant Major entered with his accustomed enthusiasm.

This expedition, numbering twenty-four persons,

amply provisioned, and destined to be the most fortunate in the annals of exploration, left the rendezvous near Mount Canobolas, on the outskirts of settlement, on the 17th of March, 1836. The first movement was made towards the old position at the station of Buree, and then the route was followed to the Lachlan. This river, as well as the Murrumbidgee, which was reached on its lower course, had previously been explored, and Mitchell had not much to add that was new or striking. When he conceived he was approaching the junction with the Murray, a depôt was formed beside an excellent sheet of water, to which the name of Lake Stapylton was given. Mitchell now divided his party, and, taking an escort, struck out boldly for the Darling, which was still 100 miles distant. The usual difficulties of this kind of travelling were encountered; but no one knew better how to overcome them than this intrepid explorer. The junction of the two chief rivers of Australia was reached without loss of time—a position which Mitchell says he recognized at once from a drawing of Captain Sturt's. This compliment Sturt duly acknowledged, remarking at the same time that it was the only praise he had ever received from Sir Thomas Mitchell, and he was afraid in this case it was not very well deserved, as the drawing had been made from a verbal description, and by an Edinburgh clergyman who had never visited Australia! The expedition was in great danger here from an exasperated tribe of blacks who kept hanging upon the rear, and only waited for an opportunity to strike a decisive blow. The aspect of matters was so threatening that Mitchell resolved to abandon the Darling, and fall back upon his alternative instructions, which directed him to explore the upper courses of the Murray. But the hostile tribe was now between his own party and the depôt, which was 100 miles away. Their number was rapidly increasing, and their attitude growing more menacing every day. A conflict could not be much longer averted, and Mitchell, as a military man, was not willing to allow the enemy to choose the most suitable time for the attack. The men under his command appear to have understood his intentions, and, without waiting for orders, fired upon the tribe. Seven were killed, and the multitude dispersed. It was a severe remedy, but also a very effectual one, for this tribe never attempted to cause them further annoyance.

On arriving at Lake Stapylton, Mitchell had the satisfaction of finding that the depôt had been unmolested, a circumstance which relieved his mind from considerable anxiety. The situation of the depôt was ascertained to be about ten miles from the junction of the Murrumbidgee with the Murray. The latter was crossed about a mile higher up, and the united exepdition started again with the intention of exploring this interesting but unknown river. From this purpose they were soon diverted by the discovery of an important tributary, which seemed to lead them into a better country than the Murray was likely to do.

After losing or leaving this creek another was discovered, of still greater importance, to which Mitchell gave the name of the Loddon, from the marked resemblance he thought it possessed to its namesake in the old home. The country consisted of open downs, and was the richest Mitchell had seen since he had left Sydney. The plains were covered with anthistirium, or kangaroo grass, which bent under the breeze like a field of oats. The country was so lightly timbered that the explorers could scarcely find fuel to make a fire at several of their places of encampment. This district also yielded many new and beautiful plants, which greatly enriched the botanical collection. Mitchell next ascended Mount Hope, a peak which he so named because he expected to obtain a view of the southern ocean from its summit. This anticipation was not realized, but he enjoyed the prospect of an unlimited reach of the class of country he had already discovered. Another hill, called the Pyramid, from its peculiar form, afforded also an excellent view, and raised in Mitchell a transport of joy. He could scarcely find words to describe the magnificence of the scene, or express the delight he felt on account of his own good fortune. "The scene," says he, "was different from anything I had ever before witnessed, either in New South Wales, or elsewhere—a land so inviting, and still without inhabitants. As I stood, the first intruder on the sublime solitude of these verdant plains, as yet untouched by flocks or herds, I felt conscious of being the harbinger of many changes there; for our steps would soon be followed by the men and the animals for which it seemed to be prepared." And again—"We had at length discovered a country ready for the immediate reception of civilized man, and fit to become eventually one of the great nations of the earth. Unencumbered with too much wood, yet possessing enough for all purposes; with an exuberant soil under a temperate climate; bounded by the sea-coast and mighty rivers, and watered abundantly by streams from lofty mountains, this highly interesting region lay before me, with all its features new and untouched as they fell from the hands of the Creator. Of this Eden it seemed I was the only Adam; and it was indeed a sort of paradise to me, permitted thus to be the first to explore its mountains and streams—to behold its scenery—to investigate its geological character—and finally, by my survey, to develop those natural advantages all still unknown to the civilized world, but yet certain to become at no distant date of vast importance to a new people." No prophet ever spoke truer words than these.

Soon after the Loddon, the Avoca and the Avon Water were discovered. These streams irrigated the same kind of country as that which had lately been traversed. This tract was evidently an exception to a rule which prevails throughout Australia. Good land is usually poorly supplied with water, while well-watered country is generally of little account in point of fertility; but here for once was a district which was equally distinguished for the abundance of its streams and the excellence of its soil. The explorers now took a direction more to the eastward, to reach a lofty mountain-chain which appeared to be about 40 miles distant. This range forms a division between the northern and the southern waters, and is really the extremity of the coast range. Mitchell called these the Grampians, from a supposed resemblance to a chain of the same name in the Southern Highlands of Scotland. Taking two of his best men, he next ascended Mount William, a peak which rises 4,500 feet above the sea and is the highest in the group. The weather being unfavourable to the object in view, it was found necessary to spend a miserably cold night upon its summit, and the exposure permanently injured the health of his two companions, who had followed the explorer on three expeditions. An excellent view was obtained at last, and another great landmark, Mount Arapiles, was fixed upon as the next object toward which they were to move. This was a bold and isolated mountain lying westward of the range. Five streams had to be crossed in passing over the intermediate tract, and these were subsequently found to unite and form the Wimmera. It was hoped this important river would lead them to the ocean, but it turned to the northward and flowed into the interior. The tract of country next discovered presented a very singular aspect. The surface, as far as the eye could reach, was studded with lakes, which differed greatly in size, but were circular in form. Their number must have been prodigious; from one point of view no fewer than twenty-seven were counted. Most of these circular lakes were brackish to the taste, and many too salt to be fit for use.

The extremity of the Grampians had now been reached, and the range was being successfully turned, when the explorers saw before them a fine open country, trending away towards the Southern Ocean. The travelling was often heavy on the soft soil, and they had to be satisfied with six miles a day as the average rate of progress; nevertheless, the object in view was being steadily accomplished, and no country was ever traversed which was richer in the charming incidents of travel. July the 31st was a red-letter day for Mitchell, for it brought the welcome discovery of a fine river, which led the party to the breakers of the Southern Ocean. Its width was 120 feet, with an average depth of 12 feet, and from first to last it continued to flow through the most picturesque scenery. The discoverer gave it the name of the Glenelg, in compliment to the Secretary of State for the Colonies. The track of the expedition kept as closely as possible to the left bank of the river, which with many windings was found to be steadily making southward. One of the most remarkable features of the Glenelg is the number of feeders which it receives from both sides of its basin. These occasionally flowed through deep ravines, which made travelling difficult for the drays. But the scenery is described as being exquisite. Mitchell put the English language on the rack to make it express his conception of the lovely scenes which daily met his eye. Either of the valleys of the Wando or the Wannon might well pass for a modern Tempé. On the 12th of August the Rifle Range was reached, and from one of the heights Mount Gambier, near Cape Northumberland, was plainly seen, and this was accepted as sufficient evidence that the sea could not be very far distant. After receiving another tributary, which was named the Stokes, the river, affected also by the proximity to the ocean, became so much increased in size as to induce Mitchell to launch the boat which had been brought from Sydney. A depôt was accordingly formed at this position which was called Fort O'Hare. Mitchell took two-thirds of his men, and, after a few days' pleasant sail, landed safely at the mouth of the Glenelg.

Before returning to Sydney it was thought advisable to make a short journey to Portland Bay, for the sake of examining the intervening country. In this excursion various streams were discovered and crossed, such as the Crawford, the Fitzroy, and the Surrey; and the prominent peaks, Ellerslie, Clay, and Kincaid, were ascended or sighted. The country generally was swampy in the flats, and poor in the higher grounds, until Portland was reached, where the soil was found to be of the best possible description. Here a great surprise was in store for the explorers. They had stumbled by mere chance on the newly-formed station of Edward Henty, from Tasmania, who generously supplied them with provisions for the homeward journey.

Going still forward, Mitchell kept for a considerable time on the southern fall of the range, in the hope of finding a pass which would be generally available. Such an opening he was fortunate enough to discover, near the foot of Mount Byng, which he safely passed through, barring an accident to his travelling gear. While this was being repaired, he made an excursion to a prominent height about 30 miles to the south, in the hope of being able to catch a glimpse of Port Phillip, and thus enable him to connect his surveys with this important position. To this height he gave the name of Mount Macedon, and from its summit was able to observe some of the topographical features of what is now the site, or the immediate neighbourhood, of Melbourne, and also white sails or tents, which most likely were the encampments of Batman and Fawkner, who had been in their new home only a few months.

In returning, the Campaspe River was discovered, and other tributaries of the Murray, made known by Hume and Hovell, were crossed without difficulty. The most serious obstacle was the passage of the Murray; but it was passed without accident or mishap, although it was 80 yards in width. Some rugged country had to be encountered before the Murrumbidgee was crossed. But this was the *ultimus labor* of the expedition, for the settled territory had now been reached. Mitchell accordingly reckoned this outpost the termination of his journey; and it had not been a short one. He had travelled over 2,400 miles of country, and was seven months in the bush. But he had been more fortunate than any of his predecessors; nor, indeed, has his success been eclipsed to this day. For this splendid service he was worthily rewarded with the honour of knighthood from the British Crown.

IV.

The good fortune which had followed Sir Thomas Mitchell throughout his three earlier expeditions did not forsake him during this one, which proved to be the last and most arduous of the series. It was his ambition this time to cross the continent and open an overland route to the distant Carpentaria. Of all men living, he was the most likely to accomplish this task. He did not, indeed, attain the desire of his heart, but in all other respects his expedition was eminently successful, and forms a memorable epoch in the history of exploration. The party mustered at the old rendezvous of Buree, in the Western District, which, though no longer the outpost of settlement, was yet a convenient starting-point. Mitchell chose for his second in command Mr. Edmund B. Kennedy, the unfortunate explorer who, several years later, was killed by the blacks when leading a disastrous expedition in Cape York Peninsula. The rest of the party were mostly convicts from Port Jackson, who had volunteered their services in the hope of obtaining their freedom. The little army, consisting of two dozen able-bodied men, amply provisioned, left Buree on the 15th of December, 1845. The old route was followed for a considerable way, and in a short time the Hervey Range, containing the sources of the Bogan, was crossed without serious difficulty. For a long distance westward the country was now occupied by squatters, but many of the outsiders had already succumbed to the hostility of the Darling blacks, who had speared their cattle and otherwise harassed them beyond the limit of human endurance. Ten years had now passed away since Mitchell led his preceding expedition through these parts, and the abortive attempts at settlement were the principal changes observable in the general aspect of the country. One very remarkable minor feature was the appearance of couch-grass and horehound, which had sprung up around the stockyards. Mitchell was quite positive in asserting that no specimen of these plants could have been found in the district before the white men settled there.

The party suffered from want of water till Nyngan was reached, on the 16th January, and then one difficulty was quickly followed by another. Most of the men were seized with eye-blight, and compelled to remain in camp longer than was convenient for the object of the expedition. But they were again on the move as soon as circumstances would permit, the march being now directed towards the Macquarie. Meanwhile an encampment was made on the Canonbar, a tributary of the Bogan. While resting here the saltbush became an object of curiosity, and some interesting experiments were made with this singular plant of the interior plains. The tiny leaves were found to be a tolerable substitute for vegetables after boiling, by which process a yield of pure salt was obtained in the proportion of one ounce to the pound. The condition of the stock also bore witness to the fattening quality of the same plant.

After a few days of eventful travel by way of Sturt's Duck Ponds, the Macquarie River was struck a few miles below Mount Harris, which had been an important landmark for explorers since the time of Oxley. The channel was dry, but the blacks reported a heavy flood as near at hand. Mitchell had often heard of sudden inundations appearing in an arid part of the country, and was anxious to witness so singular a visitation. Late in the still evening there fell upon his ear a dull murmur as of distant thunder, speedily followed by a cracking and crashing of trees, and in a few minutes more the river was overflowing its banks in a wide-spreading flood. The phenomenon is described as being grand in the extreme, and of so improbable a character as scarcely to be credited unless it had been witnessed.

On the 27th the Castlereagh was reached, and the next day the party found themselves on the banks of the Darling. For many miles in both directions the river at this period was studded with pastoral settlements. Having crossed at Warley, near one of the stations, Mitchell now struck out for the Narran, the nearest point of which was reckoned to be about

35 miles distant. The intervening space was found to consist of choice pastoral country, covered with tall kangaroo grass. Commissioner Mitchell, son of the explorer, had previously traversed these parts, and this expedition soon "pulled up" his tracks. The line of the Narran River having thus been already explored, it was traversed as expeditiously as possible, and this part of the journey was over by the beginning of April, when the Balonne (pronounced Baloon) was sighted. Mitchell described it as the finest river he had seen in Australia, with the exception of the Murray. The current was very slight, but the water stretched out in long and beautiful reaches. The march was once more resumed, and the party moved along the line of this river till St. George's Bridge was reached, where the width expanded to 120 yards. At this point there is a chain of rocks stretching from bank to bank, which has always the appearance, and sometimes the convenience, of a natural bridge. It was this circumstance which led to its being called St. George's Bridge, a name which it still retains in common with the flourishing township that has sprung up in the vicinity.

While enjoying a short interval of repose in this enchanting situation, Mitchell had the pleasure of receiving a despatch from headquarters containing a brief account of Leichhardt's successful journey to Port Essington. Being somewhat jealous of his rival, and, it may be, concerned for his own laurels, he determined on making a redoubled effort to cross the continent and discover a more practicable route than Leichhardt had been able to find. Leaving Kennedy in charge of the depôt at St. George, he took a light party and pushed forward, having given instructions to the rest to follow his tracks when the stock should be sufficiently recruited for travel. One day's march brought the advance party to the junction of another important river, which was afterwards found to be the Maranoa. But they still kept the line of the Balonne as far as the Cogoon, a considerable tributary, which was now followed. This led the explorers into a splendid district, known afterwards as the Fitzroy Downs, near the centre of which the town of Roma now stands. This fine region was studded with isolated mountain-peaks, one of which Mitchell hastened to ascend. The prospect obtained from its summit was magnificent, and the pasture so abundant on this height as to suggest the name of Mount Abundance, which it has ever since retained. At a short distance the three-peaked Bindango, standing near its fellow, Bindeygo, formed most picturesque features in the landscape. It was on Mount Abundance that the first bottle-tree was discovered. This is the strangest product of the Australian forest, and Sir Thomas was disposed to regard it as a *lusus naturæ* in the vegetable kingdom.

The telescope again brought into view a range of hills. Mitchell, bent on reaching Carpentaria, had for some time been disappointed in not finding the division of the northern waters, and fervently hoped

this distant range would prove to be the dividing
line. This watershed was to him, through the whole
journey, what the hörizon is to the traveller—always
appearing near and ever receding. Many a weary
day did he toil on, sustained by this expectation, but
it kept mocking him to the last, and he went to his
grave without having crossed the coveted watershed.
But for the present he enjoyed the pleasures of hope.
Leaving Mount Abundance he soon discovered the
Amby, which, being followed, led on to the Maranoa,
whose junction with the Balonne he had previously
discovered. Here he established another depôt and
waited for Kennedy, making in the meantime several
short excursions in various directions. Not far from
this depôt a squatting station was subsequently
formed, and more recently an important town has been
built, in both of which the name of Mitchell has been
perpetuated. Kennedy having brought up his party
in excellent condition, the experiment which had been
so successfully made at St. George's Bridge was
repeated here—the leader again setting out for the
north with a small equipment and a four months'
supply of provisions. The natives in this quarter were
not disposed to stand on friendly terms with the
strangers, and usually kept at a safe distance. One
inconvenience only Mitchell regretted. Many interesting natural features were observed, especially
mountain-peaks, which he would gladly have made
known under the aboriginal names. Failing in this,
his favourite custom, he called them after some of the

leading men of the time, as Owen, Faraday, Buckland, and P. P. King. As an exception, he named one of the heights Mount Aquarius, in remembrance of a very seasonable supply of water it had furnished for his party. This difficulty now seemed to be overcome for some time by the discovery of the Nive and the Nivelle, important tributaries of a large river. This was the Warrego, which would have been followed had it not persisted in taking a course which would have led them in the opposite direction to Carpentaria.

The country to the northward continued to rise till it reached an elevation of something like 1,500 feet. Being also of a mountainous character, it was fondly hoped that here, at least, would be found the long-sought watershed. This anticipation was rather confirmed by the discovery of a beautiful stream, now called Salvator Rosa, which flowed northward with a clear and musical current. This pleasing delusion lasted only one day, for on the morrow the lovely river ended its course in a reedy lake, on the opposite side of which a channel was found, but it contained no water at that time. This is one of the heads of the Nogoa, a river trending too much to the east to suit Sir Thomas's purpose. Other discoveries of streams or watercourses were made soon afterwards, two of the principal being named the Claude and the Balmy Creek. These designations are suggestive of pleasant associations, and, while speaking well for the country, sufficiently prove that the expedition had its share of enjoyment as well as the usual experience of toil and fatigue.

The 21st of July was rendered memorable by the discovery of the Belyando, a fine river, heading towards the north, and offering a better promise of leading to the Gulf. In this expectation, it was eagerly followed, and in four days conducted the explorers across the Tropic of Capricorn. In many parts the country was excellent, stretching out in splendid downs, which squatters have long since applied to a lucrative purpose, but in other places the axe had to be used to clear a path through the brigalow scrubs. In common with other explorers, Mitchell has noticed that "the Australian rivers have all distinguishing characteristics, which they seem to possess from their source to their termination." The Belyando was no exception. It was found throughout its course to have an unfortunate propensity for splitting into channels, which were often difficult to trace through the thick scrub; but, as a compensation, these branches afforded excellent facilities for storage of water against dry seasons. Many days of persevering travel gave the party a good northing, but, after passing over three and a half degrees of latitude, it began to be evident that the Belyando also was going to deceive them. It had been steadily, and latterly very decisively, making for the east, thus leaving no hope of conducting the expedition to Carpentaria. Mitchell rightly conjectured that it must be the tributary which Leichhardt had seen joining the

Suttor, and, with a crushing feeling of disappointment, determined to change his front and return home.

Having still a sufficient store of provisions, he was unwilling to continue his homeward track, and resolved to follow up a river to the westward, which took its rise in the high ground previously mentioned. It was found to lead through first-class pasture land, and this excursion resulted in opening up a large area of squatting country. Many tributaries were noticed to fall in on either side, particularly the Alice, which came from the north. The main river was followed till it, too, left no hope of leading to the coveted north. Soon after Sir Thomas gave up the search altogether, and set his face in earnest for the settled districts, which he reached, after no long interval, by way of the Mooni River and the Liverpool Plains. Having failed to enter into communication with the aborigines, he was unable to ascertain the native name of the river which had led him so far to the west. It was the last of his great discoveries, and he called it after the name of the Queen, an unfortunate designation, as there is another Victoria River on the west coast. About the same period Captain Sturt was exploring on another part of this river, and gave it the name of Cooper's Creek. The natives called it the Barcoo, and by this name it is now generally known throughout its whole course.

CHAPTER IX.

KENNEDY'S DISASTROUS EXPEDITION TO CAPE YORK.

THIS chapter is from first to last a tale of woe. The history of exploration, tragic as it has so often been, contains no parallel to the expedition which is now to be described. Of the thirteen brave men who, full of hope, set forth on this memorable journey, only three starved and emaciated shadows of humanity returned to tell the story of their miserable sufferings. The disaster produced in Sydney an impression which was the more saddening as a successful issue had been confidently expected. The leader, Mr. Edmund B. Kennedy, was supposed to be a thoroughly capable person. He had formerly been taken from the Survey Department and placed second in command of the northern expedition of Sir Thomas Mitchell, whose discoveries on the Barcoo and the Warrego he had subsequently followed up on his own account. So great care had been taken in selecting the most promising leader, for this reason, simply, that the colony was now passionately in earnest on this business. The rising importance and threatening attitude of Port Phillip made it more than ever necessary to discover, if possible, a practicable route to some northern port which might serve as an *entrepôt* for the trade with India. Mitchell, after doing his best, had failed to supply this want. Leichhardt had, indeed, been more successful, for he had actually reached Port Essington; but his track was too rough and circuitous to serve the purpose of commerce. Another effort to reach the same object was now to be made on a modified plan. To simplify the process, it was proposed to land a party of explorers at Rockingham Bay, with instructions to proceed overland to Port Albany, near Cape York, in the extreme north. This was the primary object, and if it could be attained, other advantages might follow in the opening up of new country, and the eventual connection of the survey with those of Leichhardt and Mitchell.

The enterprise commenced with unfavourable omens. The voyage to Rockingham Bay was tempestuous, and extended over the unusual period of twenty-one days. By the 1st day of June, 1848, the adventurers had escaped from the perils of the sea, and committed themselves to the guardianship of a land inhabited as yet only by savages. A hazardous journey of six months lay between them and Port Albany, while their only resource against starvation consisted of 1 ton of flour, 90 lbs. of tea, and 600 lbs. of sugar, together with a few sheep, which were soon almost wholly lost. It was arranged that a relief vessel should be waiting at Cape York to receive the explorers at the end of their journey, and it was promised also that an attempt would be made to communicate with them at Princess Charlotte Bay, if they could engage to reach that place by the month of August. With these arrangements and understandings the *Tam o' Shanter* spread sail, and left Kennedy with his heroic dozen to battle with difficulties, known and unknown, as they best could. These unhappily commenced at once, and never ceased till nearly all this brave band found rest in the arms of death. The ground on which the landing had been effected was covered with interminable swamps, and five precious weeks were spent in turning these, before any northing could be made. It was the misfortune of this ill-provisioned party to encounter within a short compass nearly all the obstacles which have beset Australian explorers, and these, truly, have been neither few nor small. Scarcely had the maze of marshes been left behind when impenetrable thickets threatened to bar further progress. These first visitors to York Peninsula found the scrubs entangled and interlaced by a new creeper which is now known under the name of *Calamus Australis*, and this novelty proved to be a scourge of the first magnitude. For days in succession the axe had to be used to cut a passage through this exquisite specimen of nature's lattice-work, and then the severed tendrils, furnished as they were with curved spines, and made the plaything of the wind, kept hooking the flesh of the men at work, who were thus subjected to perpetual annoyance. But a more serious enemy now began to hang upon the rear. The blacks, having assumed a threatening attitude for some time past, at last appeared in strong force, painted and armed for the fight. Outward signs of friendship were still kept up; but it was too evident that they were bent on mischief, and only waited a fit opportunity for a decisive assault. When least expected a spear was thrown into the camp, which Kennedy determined to accept as a challenge, and gave battle. This decision was exceedingly unfortunate, as it led to extremities at once. Men like Sturt would have tried every conceivable shift before allowing matters to come to the *dernier ressort*, and might have gained their object by the mere sound of a gun. But Kennedy ordered his men to load and fire upon the savages at once. Four or five of the ringleaders fell, and the rest retreated for the present; but only to nurse their wrath and meditate revenge. Here was the beginning of another train of sorrows, for the barbarians never ceased to dog Kennedy's steps till their enmity was quenched in his blood.

The progress of the expedition was slow and unsatisfactory. Cases of individual sickness occasioned irritating delays, and physical hindrances became more frequent than ever. A considerable part of the route lay between the spurs of the range which would have to be crossed before Cape York was reached. It was with great difficulty that the drays carrying the provisions had been brought over the rugged country, and it had sometimes been necessary to lower them into the ravines by means of ropes. As the journey ahead looked still more precipitous, it was judged impracticable to take them much further, and with great reluctance Kennedy resolved on exchanging this mode of conveyance for pack-horses. Everything that could be spared was accordingly abandoned, for the animals were now too poor to carry heavy loads. In this manner and under such difficulties a fresh start was made. Amid so many discouragements only one gleam of hope sustained the heroic adventurers. They were now nearing Princess Charlotte Bay, the appointed rendezvous for themselves and the succour which was promised from the sea. But they had been delayed too long to admit of this assistance being confidently relied on. August was fixed as the time of meeting, but October had now come, and they began to be uneasy lest the vessel should have given them up and returned. These fears, as the issue proved, were only too well founded. The hapless wanderers, standing on the precipices of the range, scanned the inhospitable coast for miles around this lonely trysting-place; but instead of the wished-for help, now a question of life and death, they were met by nothing but blank despair. With heavy hearts the explorers again set their faces towards Cape York, now knowing for certain that they must either reach this goal or lay their bones in the wilderness. Unhappily, the difficulties of travel thickened more and more, and it became painfully evident to Kennedy that he would have to leave the greater part of his men and strike out with all speed, in the hope of returning with assistance. Provisions, too, had become alarmingly short, and under any circumstances starvation seemed all but inevitable. The camp was now on Puddingpan Hill, in the vicinity of Weymouth Bay, and it was determined to leave eight men in this depôt for the present. All the provisions that could be spared were 28 lbs. of flour and a couple of horses, which were only walking skeletons. Kennedy reckoned on reaching Port Albany in about a fortnight, and started with a light party of four men, including an aboriginal of tried fidelity named Jacky Jacky. The remainder of this history is derived from the barely intelligible language of poor Jacky. It appears that for the first three weeks very unsatisfactory progress was made, much precious time being lost in consequence of a gun accident. One of the men being thus rendered unfit for travel, and another required to nurse him, Kennedy resolved to divide his party a second time. He accordingly left three men near Shelborne Bay, and, with only Jacky to accompany him, determined to make a life-and-death struggle to bring succour from Port Albany. But his own strength was rapidly failing, and the hostility of the blacks, who had so long hung upon his rear, was daily assuming a more deadly aspect. This misfortune was the more to be regretted as this tedious and toilsome journey was almost at an end. From one of the heights Kennedy caught a glimpse of Port Albany, with its neighbouring island, and pointed them out to his dusky companion. But his life's journey was still nearer its close. The blacks were gathering in hundreds. An ineffectual attempt was tried to elude their vigilance

by camping in the scrub without a fire, but they again
made their presence known by hurling the deadly
spear. Jacky made a rush to rally the horses, which,
frantic with their wounds, had begun to dash through
the scrub, and, on returning, found his master had
been speared, surrounded, and robbed. A feeble
resistance was offered to the assault of the savages,
but it had little effect, and was soon over. Jacky
thought Kennedy was dying fast, and asked if he
was now going to leave him. He said he was fatally
wounded, and, having given a brief order concerning
his papers, breathed his last in the arms of his faithful
attendant. Such was the end of Mr. E. B. Kennedy,
a man who has left his mark on our history, and will
be honoured by posterity as one of the most heroic,
if not the most judicious, and certainly the least
fortunate, of the Australian explorers.

Jacky, being now alone, and more dead than alive,
made his way as best he could to Port Albany. His
progress was sometimes less than a mile per day, but
he struggled on in the hope of finding the promised
vessel. Almost six months had passed away since the
party of thirteen disembarked at Rockingham Bay.
It was within two days of Christmas, and those in
charge of the ship were debating with themselves
whether it was worth while waiting any longer, when
a poor emaciated creature was observed to drag himself from the forest and make signs to the vessel.
Being conveyed on board, his tale of woe was soon
told, in such words as he could use. The gravity of

the situation became apparent immediately, and the order was given at once to hoist sail for Shelborne Bay, in the hope of being able to rescue the three men who had been left at Pudding-pan Hill. The search was unsuccessful. No trace of these unfortunates could then, or has ever since been discovered. There still remained the depôt at Weymouth Bay, where the necessities of the eight men left there could not be otherwise than urgent in the extreme, if they were still alive. All haste was made to the rescue. The eight were all found, but six of them were dead. The two survivors were more like ghosts than human beings of flesh and blood. The tale of miseries which they had to relate was heartrending. In addition to the lingering horrors of starvation, they had to endure incessant attacks from the blacks, who, knowing they had them in their power, enjoyed a savage delight in prolonging the distress of their victims. Yet it appears that the half-dozen eventually died of hunger, a fate which the survivors must inevitably have shared if relief had been much longer delayed. Having been too weak to bury their dead companions, this sacred duty was performed by the ship's crew, who thereafter hastened homeward with the miserable remains of Kennedy's heroic but ill-starred expedition.

CHAPTER X.

LEICHHARDT'S EXPEDITIONS TO PORT ESSINGTON AND INTO THE INTERIOR.

Dr. Ludwig Leichhardt, who was born in Germany and educated in France, came to Australia in the year 1840. He commenced his career in Sydney as a lecturer on botany, his favourite science, and became immediately popular. Naturally fond of travel, and being eager for enterprise, Leichhardt took to the bush, where he earned his fame and lost his life. His first essays in exploration were made in the country lying between Brisbane and Wide Bay, which he traversed specially in the interests of botanical and geological science. In these adventures he was associated for the most part with the blacks, who welcomed him as a benefactor on account of his medical skill, of which he gave them the full benefit without fee or reward.

Having accomplished his object in this part of the country, Leichhardt returned to Sydney, where he found public opinion strongly excited on the question of exploration. Sir Thomas Mitchell, having led three expeditions into the interior with great success, was mainly instrumental in creating this outburst of enthusiasm, which called for other enterprises of a like nature and purpose. At this period, also, a keen desire was manifested for an overland route to Carpentaria as a highway, so far, to India, which was supposed to offer an unlimited market for Australian horses. Already a settlement had come into existence at Port Essington, which was reckoned a suitable *entrepôt* for the prospective traffic. The one thing wanted was an overland route to this place, and it was generally thought the time had come when an attempt should be made to discover it. Sir Thomas Mitchell was again to the front, expressing himself ready for the undertaking, with Dr. Leichhardt as second in command. He had already arranged to proceed to his old depôt at Fort Bourke and to strike north for Carpentaria. But a fatal obstacle was unexpectedly interposed. Sir George Gipps, being in a bad humour with his advisers, refused to confirm the vote for supplies which the Council had unanimously passed, and, as a natural consequence, the whole project fell to the ground. This was a sore blow to Leichhardt, but it did not unman him. Despairing of help or countenance from the Governor, he volunteered to lead an expedition to Port Essington on his own account if private liberality should prove itself equal to the occasion. In a very short time sufficient resources were forthcoming, and Leichhardt now set himself to redeem his promise.

I.

In this expedition it was resolved to start from Moreton Bay and keep the eastern fall of the main range, thus avoiding the parched-up interior and following a route which was likely to furnish an adequate supply of water. Leichhardt could never have been far beyond the reach of the sea-breeze—a circumstance which caused Mitchell to speak of him, rather contemptuously, as a "timid coaster." The party, consisting of ten persons, with seven months' provisions, made an auspicious start from Brisbane, and had reached the outskirts of settlement by the 1st of October, 1844. Crossing the Darling Downs, the River Condamine was followed as far as practicable, after which a dividing range was traversed and the Dawson River discovered. It flowed through a magnificent valley, which was soon after proved to be an excellent pastoral district. When it turned too much to the east a more northerly course was steered, which led to the discovery of Palm-Tree Creek, in a splendid valley abounding in palms, and hence the name. The next stage was much impeded by brigalow scrub, but a succession of lagoons supplied the party with plenty of water and excellent game. Zamia Creek followed in the line of discovery, bounded by the Expedition Range, which was crossed, and Comet Creek discovered soon after. This latter led on to the Mackenzie, which had to be abandoned in a short time, as it flowed too much to the east. The picturesque Peak Range was now passed. The mountains not only appeared magnificent in point of scenery, but were believed also to contain precious stones. Leichhardt says:—"A profusion of chalcedony and fine specimens of agate were observed in many places along the basaltic ridges." On the 13th of February they discovered an important river, which was named the Isaacs, but it was not followed, as the course was again directed towards the mountains. Shortly after they had the good fortune to come upon the Suttor, which brought them to the Burdekin. This was the best discovery yet made, as it served them for a guide over more than two degrees of latitude. When this river also left them for the coast, their route was directed more inland, with a view of reaching Carpentaria. In this cross-country journey a conspicuous mountain observed in the distance received the name of Mount Lang, "after Dr. Lang, the distinguished historiographer of New South Wales." A few unimportant creeks having been crossed, they found themselves on the western fall, and discovered one of the Gulf rivers, which was named the Lynd. Here, and at several later camps, the explorers were treated with a visit from some awfully pertinacious intruders. "We had scarcely left our camp," says Leichhardt, "when swarms of crows and kites took possession of it, after having given us a fair fight during the previous days whilst we were drying the meat. Their boldness was, indeed, remarkable; and if the natives had as much we should soon have to quit our camps." In this district a botanical novelty, in the form of a bread-fruit tree, was found, and used to some advantage. As the Lynd did not lead in the most suitable direction, it was left, and a straight line

taken to the Gulf. This was the occasion of the
discovery of another river, which was called the
Mitchell, in honour of the distinguished explorer; but
it, too, was given up for a shorter course. In this
quarter a deplorable accident occurred. The camp
was attacked during night by the blacks, when
Gilbert, the naturalist to the expedition, was killed.
From this point the journey was continued round the
head of the Gulf. Numerous rivers were crossed,
some of which had been long before discovered by
exploring navigators, and others were now for the
first time brought to light. Among the latter were
the Gilbert and the Roper, both receiving names in
honour of members of the expedition. The Roper
River had many tributaries, one of which was called
Flying-Fox Creek, from the myriads of these
creatures which had chosen it for their haunt.
Leichhardt says:—" I went with Charley and Brown
to the spot where we had seen the greatest number of
flying-foxes, and whilst I was examining the neighbouring tree, my companions shot 67, of which 55
were brought to our camp, which served for dinner,
supper, and luncheon." By the 24th of November the
expedition had crossed the watershed between the
streams flowing into the Gulf and those heading for
the Indian Ocean. After much toilsome travel, the
South Alligator River was reached, about 60 miles
from its mouth and 140 from Port Essington. In this
locality the waterfowl are described as being seen, not
in crowds, but in "clouds." "Here," says Leichhardt,

"we should have been tolerably comfortable but for a large green-eyed fly, which was extremely troublesome to us, and which scarcely allowed our poor horses to feed." In order to avoid some bad, rocky ground, the party turned to the south and struck the East Alligator River. The last stage of the journey was travelled under the direction of a native guide, and the goal of the expedition reached in safety. After a month's rest in this settlement, Leichhardt found a schooner bound for Port Jackson, and embraced this opportunity of returning to Sydney by sea. His unexpected appearance there seemed like an apparition from the other world. For a long time he had been given up for lost, and a search expedition had already come back unsuccessful. The citizens of Sydney at once instituted a public subscription for Leichhardt and his associates, who had thus travelled over 3,000 miles in fifteen months. The amount reached the figure of £1,500, which was supplemented by a Government grant of £1,000. The Royal Geographical Societies, also, hastened to show their appreciation of the explorer's labours by presenting him with their gold medals. These rewards had been as honestly earned as they were handsomely made. The route he had laid open was, indeed, useless for the purpose intended, as being impracticable for traffic, and inferior to others which have since been discovered, but the expedition brought to the knowledge of the colonists an immense extent of excellent country, which was speedily occupied by pastoral tenants.

II.

A short period of repose sufficed to recruit the wearied explorer and brace him up for future effort. Now more enthusiastic than ever, Leichhardt conceived the heroic idea of traversing the entire continent at its greatest width, starting from Moreton Bay and proceeding through the deserts to Swan River in Western Australia. He was now in possession of some private means, and his zeal was again supported by numerous friends. This new expedition consisted of nine persons, and his equipment, especially under the head of live stock, was provided on the largest scale the colony had yet witnessed. These consisted of 108 sheep, 270 goats, 40 bullocks, 15 horses, and 15 mules. His plan was to follow his former route for a few hundred miles, and then bear off to the westward. All went tolerably well till the Dawson country was passed, after which wet weather became a serious hindrance. At Comet Creek the party began to suffer from fever and ague, but still pushed on to the Mackenzie, where they found themselves in a deplorable plight. The resources had been wasted, not so much as a dose of medicine being left for the sick. No one being able to attend to the sheep and cattle, the whole were irretrievably lost. It now became evident to Leichhardt, as it had been for some time to his companions, that it would be the part of madness to attempt the unknown desert so ill-furnished with supplies. Conquered by dire necessity, Leichhardt returned home with a heavy heart, after a fruitless journey of seven months. The expedition had proved a total failure, and, as the old track had been followed, the journey added nothing to what was already known of the distant parts of the country.

III.

In the meantime Sir Thomas Mitchell had made a fourth exploring expedition, and on this occasion had done his best to discover an interior route to Carpentaria. He failed, however, in this object; but in all other respects the undertaking had been eminently successful. In one quarter the tracks of the two explorers had approached within a short distance of one another, and Leichhardt, being in possession of a considerable salvage from the wreck of his second expedition, proposed to examine the intervening district—a fine territory, now known as the Fitzroy Downs. This was a small undertaking for so great an explorer. Nor was it a very necessary one either, for the squatters were already in possession of the country, and the crack of the stockman's whip suggested to Leichhardt the propriety of returning home and preparing for an enterprise more worthy of his well-won reputation.

IV.

Arrangements were again made in earnest for crossing the continent to Swan River, all being ready to set out from Moreton Bay with a party of only six men, provisioned for a journey which was calculated to extend over two or three years. The second in command was one Classan, brother-in-law to Leichhardt, who had just arrived from Germany to join the expedition. The late Rev. W. B. Clarke, being surprised at so peculiar an arrangement, asked the "new chum" what qualifications he possessed for the most perilous enterprise hitherto attempted in Australia? Classan replied that he was a seaman who had suffered shipwreck, and was, therefore, well fitted to endure hardship! In this expedition Leichhardt resolved to abandon his old route for that of Sir Thomas Mitchell, which he proposed to follow as far as the bend of the Victoria (Barcoo), and then turn westward. He seems to have fallen into this track near Mount Abundance, in the neighbourhood of the present town of Roma, in Queensland. It is not possible to trace the expedition much further, nor is there any hope of the veil of mystery ever being lifted. Here are Leichhardt's last words to the civilized world, as written from M'Pherson's station, on the Cogoon, under date of 3rd April, 1848:—"I take the last opportunity of giving you an account of my progress. In eleven days we travelled from Mr. Burrell's station, on the Condamine, to Mr. M'Pherson's, on the Fitzroy Downs. Though the country was occasionally very difficult, yet everything went on very well. My mules are in excellent order, my companions in excellent spirits. Three of my cattle are footsore, but I shall kill one of them to-night, to lay in our necessary stock of dried beef. The Fitzroy Downs, on which we travelled for about 22 miles from east to west, is, indeed, a splendid region, and Sir Thomas Mitchell has not exaggerated their beauty in his account. The soil is pebbly and sound, richly grassed, and, to judge from the myalls, of the most fattening quality. I came right on to Mount Abundance and passed over a gap in it with my whole train. My latitude agreed well with Mitchell's. I fear that the absence of water in the Fitzroy Downs will render this fine country, to a great degree, unavailable. I observe the thermometer daily at 6 a.m. and 8 p.m., which are the only convenient hours. I have tried the wet thermometer, but am afraid my observations will be very deficient. I shall, however, improve on them as I proceed. The only serious accident that has happened was the loss of a spade, but we were fortunate enough to make it up at this station. Though the days are still very hot, the beautiful clear nights are cool and benumb the mosquitoes, which have ceased to trouble us. Myriads of flies are the only annoyance we have. Seeing how much I have been favoured on my present progress, I am full of hopes that our Almighty Protector will allow me to bring my darling scheme to a successful termination." This last communication, unfortunately, says nothing about the direction in which he intended to travel, and his route henceforth is a matter of pure conjecture. After years of weary waiting Mr. Hovenden

Hely was sent to search for his tracks, but without avail. Hely was played upon by the blacks, who pretended to show him several of Leichhardt's camping grounds, and finally the bones of the murdered party. They turned out, however, to be mutton-bones, and the search ended in nothing. Mr. A. C. Gregory, himself a distinguished explorer, led two expeditions with the same object in view, and discovered a tree marked "L," which may or may not have been made by Leichhardt. Walker, when searching for Burke and Wills, believed he had found some traces of the missing expedition; but these marks were again successfully contested by Landsborough. Still later a Mr. Skuthorpe, in a most mercenary fashion, tried to persuade the public, and especially the Government of New South Wales, that he had discovered certain relics of the expedition, including Leichhardt's journal in good preservation; but the affair was looked upon as an imposition, and nothing further has transpired. It cannot be said with certainty that a single trace of Leichhardt has been discovered since he wrote his letter from the Fitzroy Downs.

CHAPTER XI.

MR. A. C. GREGORY'S EXPEDITION TO THE NORTH-WEST INTERIOR.

THE part of the continent which shall next engage our attention is the north-west interior. Up to this period of our history very little had been known of this quarter, except along the seaboard and, in sparse places, for a few miles inland. The Victoria had been discovered in 1840 by Captain Stokes, who described it as a rival to the Murray, and, moreover, sailed up its channel for 50 miles without reaching the head of the navigation. By this waterway it was thought possible to reach the north-western interior, in which some traces of Leichhardt might be met with. The conduct of this expedition was entrusted to Mr. A. C. Gregory, a very capable explorer, and a man of scientific attainments. His party numbered eighteen persons, including his brother, Mr. H. Gregory, Mr. Wilson, geologist, and the now famous Baron Von Mueller as botanist. The party took with them 50 horses and 200 sheep. The *Tom Tough* and the *Monarch* landed the expedition on the Plains of Promise, near the head of the Gulf of Carpentaria, on the 24th September, 1855. The *Monarch* then returned to Moreton Bay, while the *Tom Tough* sailed round to the Victoria, having received orders to wait for the rest of the party, who were to proceed overland. In six days they made the Macadam Range, and in eight more came on to the Fitzmaurice River. At this camp the horses, which had already been greatly reduced in number, were bitten by alligators, and three of them died. On reaching the Victoria the *Tom Tough* was not to be seen, as she had been driven ashore elsewhere and had sustained severe injury. On the 3rd of January, 1856, Mr. Gregory started with eight men and followed up the Victoria for 100 miles. In latitude 16° 26′ S. it split into two branches, each of which was in succession traced up to the vanishing point. The explorers then struck forth into the desert, proceeding on a southerly course. A journey of 300 miles brought them, on the 22nd of February, to a promising creek, to which they gave the name of Sturt, in memory of the eminent explorer. To their intense disappointment, this clue also failed them, for Sturt's Creek finally resolved itself into a sheet of salt water, to which they gave the appropriate designation of Lake Termination. Two mountains in this neighbourhood were called Mount Mueller and Mount Wilson, after the botanist and the geologist of the expedition. Once more the terrible salt desert lay before the baffled explorers. "Nothing," says the leader, "could have been more forbidding than the long, straight lines of drift-sand which, having nearly an east and west direction, rose beyond each other like the waves of the sea; and though the red glare of the sand was partially concealed by a scanty growth of spinifex, the reflection from its surface caused the passing clouds to be coloured a deep purple. We had long passed the limit to which the tropical rains of the north-west coast extend, and the country south of 19° seemed only to be visited by occasional thunderstorms. Thus for a few miles the grass would be fresh and green, then there would be a long interval of dry, parched country, where no rain appeared to have fallen for a twelve-month. The channel of the creek also decreased in size, and the frequent occurrence of salicornia indicated the saline nature of the soil; the water became brackish, then salt, and finally spread out and terminated in the dry bed of a salt lake, a mile in diameter, which communicated with a second, of larger size, nine miles long and five wide. Though now quite dry, there were marks of water having stood for considerable periods, of from 10 to 15 feet deep, as the shells of mussels in their natural position were abundant more than a mile from the ordinary bank of the lake, showing that a large tract of country is sometimes inundated. As the mussels are a species which live in fresh water, it is evident that at such times the lake is not salt, but it would appear that as the waters evaporate and recede they become saline, as the shells found within the limits of the lake were of other species which affect brackish or salt water." One more attempt to make for the south proved abortive, and, with many regrets, Gregory returned to the depôt, after having penetrated within 730 miles of Sturt's most advanced camp towards the centre of Australia.

Falling back upon alternative instructions, the leader now left the Victoria, and, making his way across Arnheim's Land, reached the River Roper. The track of Leichhardt round the southern shores of the Gulf was followed for the most part. The Plains of Promise were crossed, but Gregory scarcely agreed with Stokes in his unqualified praise of this country. From the Albert River he resolved to seek for a better track to Moreton Bay than Leichhardt's. The Flinders was reached on the 8th of September, between which river and the Gilbert some good country was discovered. The latter was traced for 180 miles of its course. The Burdekin was reached by the 16th of October, and a fortnight later its junction with the Suttor. Gregory traced the Belyando to 22°, thus connecting the routes of Mitchell and Leichhardt with his own. Passing the Mackenzie and the Comet, the Dawson River was reached by the 15th of November. The course was then made to Brisbane through the Burnett district, a journey of 400 miles. The parties in this expedition had been absent sixteen months from the haunts of civilization. They had travelled 2,000 miles by sea and 5,000 by land.

CHAPTER XII.

BURKE AND WILLS'S EXPEDITION ACROSS THE AUSTRALIAN CONTINENT.

THE golden age of Australian exploration dates from 1860. The preceding half-century is rich in heroic efforts put forth in this direction, and bears witness to many a conquest over the mysterious interior as the fruit of much self-sacrifice. Yet these results, as a class, were of a secondary character, only sometimes answering the hopes of the explorers themselves, and not doing so at all when these expectations rose to the ambition of crossing the continent. But those days of comparative failure are now over, and 1860 marks the commencement of a bright and glorious era for the explorers of this hitherto dark continent. Within the space of the next two years Australia was crossed no fewer than six times, by as many expeditions. The foremost place in time, as well as interest, belongs to Burke and Wills, and for this reason the story of their victory and sufferings will form the subject of the present chapter.

Victoria has the credit of this expedition. The movement originated in the offer of £1,000 by Mr. Ambrose Kyte, on condition of this sum being doubled by voluntary subscriptions. The terms were soon complied with, after which the Government generously came to its aid by a vote of £5,500. The arrangements were undertaken by a committee of the Royal Society, and, as the funds were ample, it was determined to equip the expedition on the most liberal scale. As a new feature in exploration, two dozen camels were imported from India, and every provision was made to secure the object on which the young colony had set its heart. The only difficulty that remained was to find a competent leader. After much delay had been occasioned through unsuccessful negotiation, the command was finally given to an enthusiastic volunteer named Robert O'Hara Burke. This remarkable man was a native of Ireland, but was educated in Belgium, and had served as an officer in the Austrian cavalry. He subsequently returned to the "Green Isle," and entered the constabulary force. Having emigrated to Australia he received a similar appointment, and held the position of inspector of police when this new honour was conferred upon him. He was a brave and generous man—few, indeed, have been more heroic and faithful—but, as he possessed little acquaintance with Australian exploration, and was destitute of special qualifications for the work, his appointment has generally been regarded as a mistake on the part of the committee. The position of second in command, with the office of astronomical observer, was conferred on William John Wills, who had been born in Devonshire as late as 1834. He came out to Australia while a mere youth, and for a time had to betake himself to the humble occupation of shepherd, but being well educated and possessing excellent gifts of head and heart, he soon rose to the position of a government surveyor, and afterwards obtained the honourable office of assistant astronomer in the Melbourne Observatory.

The expedition, when fully organized, consisted of 15 men and 24 camels, with twelve months' provisions, weighing in all 21 tons. The start was made from Melbourne on the 20th of August, 1860—an imposing spectacle, which has yet left its impression on the memories of many of the older inhabitants of that city. By the committee's direction, they were to march first to the Darling, next to the Lower Barcoo (Cooper's Creek), and then strike northward for the Gulf of Carpentaria. Melbourne had been left too late in the season, and this disadvantage was aggravated by delays occasioned by the unwieldiness of the expedition and insubordination on the part of some of the men. At length Menindie, on the Darling, was reached. The name is new in the history of exploration, but the locality is in the neighbourhood of Laidley Ponds, a quarter which was then well known to the readers of Sturt and Mitchell. Burke formed a depôt here, in which he left the greater part of his men and some beasts of burden to recruit from the fatigues of their toilsome journey. Taking Wills, together with six men and 15 camels, he made his arrangements for a quick journey across to the Barcoo. It had been his intention to follow Sturt's old track, but he was dissuaded from his purpose by a Mr. Wright, superintendent of a neighbouring pastoral station, who told him of a better route further to the north, and volunteered to conduct the party over it in person. Both the advice and the offer were accepted; nor did experience fail to justify the change of plan. Travelling was agreeable on this new route, and water found at intervals of not more than 20 miles. The march from Menindie to Torowotto was little short of a pleasure excursion, and Burke, with the generosity which was part of his nature, now associated Wright permanently with the expedition, giving him the position of third in command. Being no longer needed as a guide, he was sent back from this place to the depôt on the Darling, with orders to bring forward the heavy supplies with all convenient speed. The advance party continued their progress into the interior, and, on the 11th of November, struck the Barcoo, which was followed until a suitable place was found where they might encamp till the arrival of Wright with the remainder of the expedition. The delay proved to be longer than had been expected; and, that the time might not be altogether lost, some explorations were made in the surrounding country, and several promising routes to the Gulf were examined with little satisfactory result. Worst of all, some of the camels were lost, and although much time was consumed in the search, they were never seen again by the explorers. Wright's delay was becoming as vexatious as it seemed to be inexcusable. Six weeks had passed away since he left Burke, and yet the whole distance from Menindie to the encampment on the Barcoo had been traversed by the advance party in twenty-two days. Chafed and irritated almost to madness under the disappointment, Burke determined to endure it no longer, and resolved "to dash into the interior, and cross the continent at all hazards." For this purpose he again divided his party, taking with himself Wills and two others, named King and Gray, together with six camels, one horse, and twelve weeks' provisions. The camp was now transformed into a permanent depôt, in which were left four men, six camels, and four horses. One of the party named Brahe was put in command, with instructions to erect a stockade as a means of defence against the natives, and to detain Wright after his arrival with supplies. Burke was now entering upon the real difficulties of his gigantic undertaking, and had at command only a mere fraction of the means which he had brought out of Melbourne. But of hope and courage he had lost nothing. On the 16th of December he took leave of Brahe and his men, telling them, with his wonted generosity, that if he were not back in three months, they might consult for their own welfare as should appear to be necessary.

Burke and Wills, together with their brave companions King and Gray, now plunged into the unknown deserts and shaped their course for Carpentaria. During the earlier stage the whole party rode on the camels or the one horse that accompanied

them, but the animals got weary, and it became
necessary to trudge it on foot. Burke and Wills
walked ahead, carrying a rifle and a revolver, while
King and Gray followed with the beasts of burden.
Their progress was necessarily slow, even though they
had not encountered serious obstacles of a physical
kind. Comfort, or anything approaching to it, was
utterly unknown. Night after night the toil-worn
wanderers encamped *sub Jove frigido*, without tents
or covering of any sort. Yet these hardships were
endured without murmur or regret. Burke is reported to have said he would not care though he had
only a shirt on his back, if so be that he could cross
Australia. It is impossible to give ample details of
this northward journey, for the materials are scanty.
Burke was not much of a literary character, and
found it too irksome a task to keep a diary. Wills
was vastly superior in this respect, but yet his
journal, otherwise so satisfactory, is defective here.
This much is certain, that they pursued a north-
westerly course through the interior, by way of what
was afterwards known as M'Kinlay Range, discovering and naming Gray and Wills creeks, Mount
Standish, and other topographical positions which
have since become prominent landmarks. By the
27th of January they had crossed the northern watershed and come on to the Cloncurry, which led them
to the Flinders. This river was mistaken for the
Albert, but was scrupulously followed, in the hope
that it would lead to the Gulf. After six weeks'

absence from the Barcoo signs of the neighbourhood of the ocean began to appear. The waters of the Flinders became brackish, and gradually widened into an estuary. A sight of the ocean would have gladdened the eyes of the explorers beyond measure, but a forest of mangroves deprived them of this gratification. Nevertheless, they had reached the mouth of the Flinders, and were within the limits of the rise and fall of the tide. The object which had cost so many sacrifices was accomplished at last, *and the continent of Australia traversed from end to end.*

The condition of the explorers was now pitiable in the extreme, and never were men more in need of rest or had better deserved it; but to rest here meant to perish, for only a fag-end of the rations was left, and if they were to see the Barcoo depôt again, it must be by subsisting on the merest pittance for the next two months. For this reason no time was lost at the Gulf, and the return journey was commenced on the 21st February. The weather happened to set in wet, which was a real misfortune, as it added immensely to the inconvenience of travel, seeing their strength was almost spent. The camels broke down and had all to be abandoned except two, which were also in a weakly state. The one horse which had been brought from the depôt was killed and eaten, to save the provisions. In addition to all the other evils sickness began to affect them, and Gray was so ill that he had to be strapped on the back of a camel.

The poor fellow, driven by starvation, had lately been caught appropriating more than his share of the provisions, and was chastised by Burke for the offence— an act of discipline which might have been spared, for poor Gray was not to eat much more of the little store. Day after day he was carried forward on the journey, but each night found him getting weaker, and it was necessary to make a halt to let him die. He breathed his last in a lonely wilderness, sacrificing his life without a murmur to the cause which he loved not less than his master did. His three surviving companions mournfully buried him in the desert with such strength as was still left them, but were so exhausted with the labour of digging his grave as to require a day's rest before attempting to renew the journey. They, too, must have succumbed to their troubles but for the sustaining power of hope, which told them the longed-for depôt could not now be far distant. Other indications also pointed the same way, and in four days after leaving Gray's grave their eyes were gladdened with the sight of the familiar landmarks of the old camping ground on the Barcoo. Burke gathered up all his remaining strength and made the desert ring with "cooeys" for his former comrades, and listened for a reply; but, *horresco referens*, no response was returned but the echo of his own voice. Could it be possible that the depôt was abandoned, and the miserable men left to perish in the wilderness? The appalling thought was quickly succeeded by the experience of the more terrible reality. The place of the encampment was plainly visible, and the stockade still standing, but no human being to break the solitude. Man could not suffer a more crushing disappointment; and it is not surprising to hear that Burke now completely broke down. But, after a short interval, one ray of hope sprang up from the depth of despair. A marked tree happened to catch the eye of one of the explorers, which contained the inscription, "Dig three feet westward." Wills and King immediately began to excavate, but Burke was too much unmanned to render any assistance. The hole was found to contain a chest with some supplies and a letter of explanation. This unhappy day in the experience of the explorers was the 21st of April, and the letter was eagerly opened to ascertain what time Brahe and his men had left. The date was also the 21st of April, at noon—in fact, the ink was scarcely dry, for the letter had been written only seven hours before it fell into the hands of Burke. It stated, in explanation, that they had remained in the depot four months; that Wright had not come with the supplies from Menindie; that the blacks were troublesome and their own provisions exhausted. Moreover, as Burke had engaged to return in three months, they considered, at the end of four, that he must have perished or taken another route.

What was to be done? To remain in the abandoned depôt was to perish, for the amount of provisions could only afford a very temporary relief.

Wills recommended an immediate move in the direction of Menindie, on the track of Brahe and party; but Burke was strongly in favour of making for South Australia, whose pastoral stations now reached as far as Mount Hopeless. At first sight there seemed reason in this advice. Burke argued that it was impossible to overtake Brahe in their emaciated condition; that Menindie was 400 miles from the depôt, whereas Mount Hopeless was only 150; and that the Barcoo River might be expected to supply them with water for the most of the route. The course to Mount Hopeless was accordingly adopted. Thinking the depôt might possibly be visited by a relief party, they took the precaution of burying a letter at the foot of the marked tree, stating the direction they had taken, adding that their weak condition rendered it impossible to travel more than four or five miles a day; but, by a strange oversight, left no external indications which would lead such a relief party to conclude that the place had been visited by the explorers. Having taken the handful of provisions, Burke, Wills and King, together with the two surviving camels, started for the most northern settlement of South Australia, striving to make the shortest course, and coming on to the river only when water failed them elsewhere. One of the camels, unfortunately, got bogged, and had to be shot, after two days' labour had been spent in trying to extricate it. As much of its flesh as could be recovered was dried and added to the small and rapidly diminishing store of provisions. They managed to save a little, also, through an occasional present of fish from the native tribes, who, fortunately, were very friendly. But a great and unexpected misfortune now befell the unhappy explorers. The Barcoo, which had been reckoned on to supply them with water, split up into several channels and lost itself in the desert. One branch after another was followed for some distance, but with no other result than the consumption of their provisions and the loss of the one surviving camel. They were now reduced to dire extremity through want of both food and water, and debated with themselves whether they should continue the journey or return and encamp on the nearest waterhole in the river, and endeavour to get subsistence from the blacks. It was difficult to say how much ground had been travelled over, but they supposed it must be somewhere about 45 miles. In reality it was about double that distance; and if they could have made another good day's journey to the south they would have seen Mount Hopeless raise its friendly head above the horizon. But, by another of those fatal decisions which haunted this expedition, they resolved to abandon their journey and return to the banks of the river. Fighting against despair even yet, they conceived a faint hope that the depôt might have been visited in the interim, and Wills, with the consent and advice of Burke and King, walked back, as he was able, to see if any relief had arrived. He reached the end of his journey on the 30th of May, but found no one there, and saw no indications which could lead him to think the place had been visited since his own party had left. Sorrowful at heart, but brave in spirit to the last, Wills again retraced his steps, and returned to his companions in a very exhausted condition; but he could not have reached them at all without the help of the blacks. All three were now destitute, and, with the exception of an occasional present of fish, had nothing in the shape of provisions. But even yet there appeared to be one resort which lay between them and death by starvation. The country abounded with a plant called nardoo, the seeds of which, when pounded and baked into a cake, were eaten by the natives. The starving explorers adopted the same practice, in the hope of still further prolonging their existence. But a little experience proved that the nardoo cakes, although allaying the pangs of hunger, contained little nourishment, and the heroic sufferers had now fallen into the last stage of starvation. If they were to live at all, it was evident they must cast themselves on the blacks, and trust to their charity. Dreadful as the alternative was, they agreed to adopt it, for life is sweet, even in the wilderness. But just here an insuperable difficulty intervened, for the blacks were not at hand and had to be sought out. Burke and King had yet strength to walk a mile, or perhaps two, in a day. But poor Wills could walk no more, and yet he was willing that his companions should go and save themselves, if too late to save him. They put together a rude shelter, and left to seek the blacks, after taking a sorrowful departure, which could hardly fail to be final, for his life was visibly ebbing away. But they were not to go far. On the second day Burke succumbed, and felt his end to be at hand. He was a brave man, yet he shrank from the idea of dying alone, and entreated King to stay with him until all was over. His dying request was religiously observed by his trusty friend, who held him in his arms till he breathed his last. Seeing he could render no more assistance there, King returned to see how it was with Wills. It was all peace, for he, too, lay quietly asleep in the arms of Death. Beside his dead body lay his journal, in which he had made his last entry with his trembling hand, noting the aspect of the weather, and added, with a stroke of pleasantry even yet, that he was just like Mr. Micawber, waiting for something to turn up. Such was the end of William John Wills, the most amiable and noble-minded of Australia's explorers. His life was one of singular promise, and great things might have been expected from him had he not, unhappily, perished in his youth. He was only 27 years of age when he fell a sacrifice to the incompetency of others whom he served or trusted. The disconsolate King was now alone in the wilderness, with his dead leaders on either side of him. Having performed his last duties to the departed, as best he could, he sought and found his sable benefactors, who received him as one of themselves, and proved by their conduct that hospitality towards the distressed is a virtue which even savages can exercise.

Having seen the last of Burke and Wills, and left King safe for the present in the hands of the friendly aborigines, let us return to the Barcoo depôt, in the hope of finding some explanation of the mystery which enshrouds that most unlucky centre of operations. Brahe, as has been already noticed, took his departure on the 21st of April, bound for Menindie. He had travelled only eight days when Wright was met coming on, *at last*, with the bulk of the supplies for the expedition. After a brief consultation the two leaders resolved to come on to the Barcoo depôt, which they reached in another eight days. Burke and party had been there during the interval, but as they left no external marks, Wright and Brahe, after a few minutes' cursory examination, concluded the depôt had not been visited, and almost immediately took their departure for Melbourne, without putting themselves to the trouble of opening the hole at the foot of the marked tree, where the explorers' letter was concealed. Again the place was left without any external indications for the direction of their friends, who might return, and when the depôt was visited by Wills, about a fortnight later, he concluded, in the absence of such indications, that no one had been there since his own party left.

Almost everyone connected with this expedition is to blame in some degree for the disasters in which it ended. The committee at Melbourne went to sleep, and were aroused to vigorous action when it was too late. Burke and party were at fault in leaving the depôt for Mount Hopeless without making some external marks which might catch the eye of anyone who should come with supplies. Brahe and Wright were guilty of unpardonable neglect in finally leaving the Barcoo depôt without opening the *cache*, to see whether the depôt chest of provisions had been taken or not. But the real author of the disasters was Wright, who loitered four months at Menindie, while the heroic explorers were slowly dying of starvation. He alleged in his defence that Burke had asked him to remain until his own appointment was confirmed by the Melbourne committee. But this is extremely improbable, and is contradicted by Burke's own despatches. For the shortcomings of the others a tolerable excuse may be made, but for the cruel conduct of Wright there is neither justification nor defence, for all the evidence saddles him with the responsibility of the horrible tragedy in which this once splendid expedition closed its career.

CHAPTER XIII.

SEARCH EXPEDITIONS IN QUEST OF BURKE AND WILLS.

As time passed on and no trustworthy tidings of the missing explorers could be obtained, anxiety on the part of the Melbourne public became unbearable. An active search was demanded with an urgency which was not to be resisted. A manifold effort was soon put forth on an unprecedented scale, and in this enterprise Victoria was materially assisted by the sister colonies. This combined action marks the meridian of Australian exploration, which, when finished, left little more to be done in the eastern half of the continent. Within the space of two years—from 1860 to 1862—it was crossed no fewer than six times, in as many different directions, by exploring parties. The search expeditions all took the field about the same time. Alfred Howitt was despatched from Melbourne on the footsteps of Burke and Wills; John M'Kinlay was sent from Adelaide to search the Barcoo and surrounding districts; Frederick Walker was commissioned to start from Rockhampton and proceed to the north; while William Landsborough was instructed to begin at Carpentaria, and examine the country to the southward as far as might be necessary. With a view to the support of all these parties, as opportunity might offer, Captain Norman was sent with the *Victoria* to form a relief depôt on the Albert River, at the Gulf of Carpentaria. There are thus four search expeditions which call for a brief review.

I.

Mr. Alfred W. Howitt, son of William and Mary Howitt, so well known to the literature of their country, was sent from Melbourne to the Barcoo (Cooper's Creek), by the route which had been taken by the missing expedition. Near Swan Hill he met Brahe, returning with the intelligence that Burke and Wills had not appeared at the depôt. Proceeding by way of Menindie and Poria Creek the Barcoo was reached on the 8th September, 1861, and the depôt at Fort Wills on the 13th. The *cache*, on being opened, was found to contain papers showing that the explorers had been there since returning from Carpentaria. The members of the expedition having thereafter dispersed in different directions in quest of information, one of them soon came back with the welcome news that King had been found. The sequel had better be given in Howitt's own words:—" I immediately went across to the blacks' wurleys, where I found King, sitting in a hut which the natives had made for him. He presented a melancholy appearance, wasted as a shadow, and hardly to be distinguished as a civilized being but by the remnant of clothes upon him. He seemed exceedingly weak, and I found it occasionally difficult to follow what he said. The natives were all gathered round, seated on the ground, looking with a most gratified and delighted expression. I camped where the party had halted, on a high bank, close to the water, and shall probably remain here ten days, to recruit King before returning." The story, as given by King, is soon told. From the time he saw his companions dead to the day he was discovered by Howitt's party he had been about two months and ten days in the wilderness. He remained by himself some days before going to the blacks. Upwards of two months had thus been spent with the aborigines. Though desiring to be quit of him at first, they afterwards became very well reconciled to his company. On the whole they behaved very well to the white stranger. As soon as King was able to walk he proceeded seven miles down the creek with the relief party, and showed them the remains of Wills, which he had buried under the sand. At a distance of about eight miles further they found also the body of Burke, which was now interred with due solemnity. The object of the expedition having been thus accomplished, preparation was made for the return to Melbourne, but before starting the camp of the natives was again visited, and some presents distributed, in acknowledgment of their humane treatment of the forlorn King.

Soon after this party returned home, a second expedition was organized, under the same leader, to bring the bodies of Burke and Wills to Melbourne. After reaching the Barcoo, a considerable time was spent in the further exploration of the surrounding country. The Stony Desert was visited, and a horse captured which had been lost by Captain Sturt 18 or 19 years before. Having at length taken possession of the bodies, they first conveyed them to Adelaide, by the route which the explorers, when living, had wished in vain to travel. This part of the journey was traversed in seven days. The remains of the two men who had been the first to cross Australia were thence conveyed to Melbourne, where they were interred with every mark of respect for their noble characters, and many a token of regret for the neglect which had left them to perish in the wilderness.

II.

Although the object which called forth all the search expeditions was completely attained by the first alone, it is yet worth while to give some attention to the other three, on account of their indirect services in the work of exploration. We shall take next in order the South Australian effort. On the 16th of August, 1861, Mr. John M'Kinlay was despatched from Adelaide, with a party of 10 men, 4 camels, 24 horses, 12 bullocks, and 100 sheep. Blanchewater, 400 miles distant, was crossed at Baker's station. The journey thence to Lake Hope was made through a dry and stony country. From this part all the way to Sturt's Stony Desert the country was poor, but contained an abundance of lakes and creeks, which were well supplied with fish. Leaving a depôt at

Lake Buchanan, M'Kinlay set out for the Barcoo, again passing through a region of lakes. In the country now visited a number of natives were found wearing pieces of European clothing. A white man's grave was pointed out by the blacks and opened by the explorers. It was really Gray's grave, but they were as yet in ignorance of the true facts of the case, and were, moreover, grossly misled by the aborigines, who pointed to a lake and told them they had killed and eaten white men there. M'Kinlay, hastily concluding that this must have been the end of the missing expedition, called the place Lake Massacre, and reported accordingly to the authorities at Adelaide. Fearing that they intended to make the like quick despatch with himself and party, M'Kinlay commanded his men to fire upon them, which made the whole lot decamp. This was an unfortunate misapprehension, for the blacks, instead of meaning to be hostile, were only giving expression to their joy after a fashion of their own. It was, in fact, the same tribe that had treated King so well, and they must have been terribly surprised by such an abrupt termination to friendly intercourse. But, in the presence of such strangers as they had encountered, it was a risky thing to boast of killing and eating white men. Having returned to the depôt on Lake Buchanan, and thence sent to Blanchewater for supplies, M'Kinlay received correct information regarding the fate of the missing expedition. There was, therefore, no need of doing anything more in this connection; but, being well supplied with all necessaries, he wisely resolved to continue his journey of exploration across the continent. On the 17th of December they were again on the march, heading in a north-easterly direction, which led them through a country barren in soil, but abounding in lakes much frequented by waterfowl. These lakes were quite as much a distinguishing feature of this region as the springs had been of the country discovered by M'Douall Stuart to the east of Lake Eyre —soon to be noticed. Further travelling was rendered difficult, first by excessive rain, and next by intolerable heat. Christmas Day was spent at a splendid lake, called Jeannie, which was found to be the haunt of innumerable waterfowl. Here many natives were observed pounding the nardoo seed between two stones, which was then baked and roasted on the ashes. At this camping-ground good feed was found for the stock, and the men also were supplied with abundance of fish by the blacks. During the night their sable neighbours proved rather too noisy, but when a rocket was sent up it had the effect of causing a dead silence till morning. The next stage led on to another lake, but it was through a country containing little vegetation except polygonum, samphire, and saltbush. One journey more brought them to a magnificent lake, which M'Kinlay called the Hodgkinson, after the second leader of the expedition. A three-days' excursion from this centre ended in the discovery of quite a number of lakes, abounding in excellent fish. The expedition had now spent four months in a region of lakes, full or dry, with many creeks and flooded hollows. This was a great surprise in a country which bordered so closely on Sturt's Stony Desert, and is still one of the enigmas of the physical geography of Australia. On the 6th of January a fresh departure was made for the north, but, after weeks of fruitless toil in the midst of a drought, a return had to be made to Lake Hodgkinson, where it was resolved to remain in camp till rain fell. During this enforced delay M'Kinlay, unable to brook idleness, took a small party and made an assault on Sturt's Stony Desert, intimating that he might be absent for three weeks. Four days proved to be quite enough, as he met with nothing but dry lakes, red sand-hills, and bare stones, although he had penetrated 57 miles into this solitude. Having returned to the camp there was nothing but the unpleasant experience of waiting for rain, while the provisions were running down with an uncomfortable rapidity. Here, too, the blacks, presenting themselves in companies of 400 or 500, were anything but agreeable neighbours. The explorers also had to put up with heat, flies, ill-health, and all manner of inconveniences, till the 10th of February, when rain came and released them from confinement. They had now to flounder in the mud through a country which is described as utterly bare of grass, like a field which had been ploughed and harrowed, but not sown. On the 13th an old camp of Burke's was passed, and by the 7th of next month Sturt's Stony Desert was left behind their backs. Towards the middle of

March some tracts of well-grassed country were reached, and named the Downs of Plenty. During the remainder of this month, also, they traversed a tolerably good country, which seemed, however, to be bordered by deserts. Tropical Australia was now entered upon, and during the whole of April the course lay through the most luxuriant vegetation. About the beginning of May the track of Burke on the Cloncurry was crossed. The Leichhardt River was reached during the same month. Here the country was simply magnificent, the grass being up to the horses' necks. Another stage brought the expedition to Stokes's Plains of Promise. Finally, on the 18th, they advanced to the tidal waters of the Gulf of Carpentaria, but dense forests of mangrove forbade their approach to the shore. Under date of the 19th of May, and while resting in the 60th camp, M'Kinlay wrote as follows:—" I consider we are now about four or five miles from the coast. There is a rise in the river here of six and two-thirds feet to-day, but yesterday it was a foot higher. Killed the three remaining sheep, and will retrace our steps on the 21st." These were the last of the 100 sheep which were started with the expedition. M'Kinlay had the credit of being the first to take sheep across the continent of Australia. They now made for the coast of the Pacific, which was struck at Port Denison, but not till a thousand obstacles were overcome and nearly all the camels and horses eaten to keep themselves alive.

III.

On the same errand Mr. Frederick Walker, Commander of Native Police, was sent from Rockhampton to the Albert River by the Queensland authorities. Taking a party of mounted troopers, he proceeded to Bauhinia Downs, on the Dawson, where the expedition was finally organized on the 7th September, 1861. The River Nogoa was reached on the 16th, after which he pushed on through Walker's Pass to the River Nivelle. By the 27th he had made the Barcoo, which was followed down for three days, during which traces both of Gregory and Leichhardt were discovered. From the Barcoo a passage was made to the Alice through much spinifex country. After crossing the watershed between the Alice and the Thomson, a fine tributary of the latter, called the Coreenda, was met with. By the 16th of October they had got into a country of high mountains, where the natives were observed to be armed with iron axes and tomahawks. Some traces of Leichhardt were also found in this quarter. The advance was now continued through a hilly country in a north-west direction to lat. 21°, where they fell in with the head-waters of the Barkly, a large tributary, or a main section, of the Flinders River, which led them through splendid country. Another fine tributary of the Flinders was soon after discovered, and called the Norman, in honour of the captain of that name who was in command of the depôt on the Albert. Nothing further of special interest occurred till the 30th of October, when they were attacked by a large party of armed natives. Walker commanded his men to fire upon them, when a dozen of these unfortunate creatures fell under his guns. There is reason to fear that the leader's experience as an officer of black troopers had led him to hold the lives of the aborigines too cheap and to forget that they were human beings, of the same blood and brotherhood as ourselves. The explorers now followed the Norman River, but had to dig in its channel for water. On the 25th of November they reached the junction of the Norman and the Flinders, the latter of which being a large and beautiful river. Here the track of Burke and Wills was discovered, leading south, but could not be followed till fresh supplies were obtained from the depôt on the Albert. Early in December the expedition came on to the Leichhardt, and then to the Albert River, the latter flowing over plains and flooded low flats, where the tracks of several other explorers were seen. On the 7th the depôt was reached and found to be under the superintendence of Captain Norman. Walker had thus made the journey in three months and twelve days from Rockhampton. In point of celerity, our annals of exploration contain nothing to beat this record. After passing thirteen days at the depôt, Walker started anew to follow up the track of Burke and Wills which he had been fortunate enough to discover. He succeeded in running it southward to the ninth camp of the missing expedition, when it ceased to be discernible, in consequence of the abundance of vegetation and the obliterating action of floods. Thinking Burke had turned off to make for the east coast, Walker altered his course to the same quarter, and made a vain attempt to follow him up. After much harassing travel he struck the Burdekin River, at Strathalbyn station, where his troubles came to an end. Making next for Port Denison, he proceeded thence to Rockhampton, which was reached on the 5th of June. The journey had thus occupied five months and two weeks. Burke and Wills were not found, of course, but much good country was discovered and the geography of Northern Australia materially advanced.

IV.

The last of these efforts to bring relief to the missing explorers was Mr. William Landsborough's expedition. The honour of being a *search* party has frequently been denied to this enterprise. Landsborough was plainly accused of having interested objects in view; and it must be confessed that his journal contains little to refute this charge, for it scarcely ever alludes to Burke and Wills, nor would any reader be likely to suspect that its author was in search of anyone in particular. Be this as it may, in cannot be doubted that, in all other respects, this expedition was a most fortunate one, and excelled all the rest in the extent of fine country which it brought to light. To the leader himself it must have seemed more like a vacation tour than a perilous journey through an unknown land. With a party of three white men and three blacks, Landsborough sailed from Moreton Bay to Carpentaria on the 24th of August, 1861. Starting from the shores of the Gulf, he explored the Albert River, under different names, for about 120 miles. This tract of country being exceedingly dry, and the blacks troublesome, he was compelled to return to the depôt on the Albert. Captain Norman told him that Walker had been there reporting the discovery of Burke's track on the Flinders. This route was accordingly followed from the Gulf to the source of the river, but neither the tracks of Walker nor Burke were found. After leaving the Flinders, the Thomson was followed, and then Cooper's Creek (Barcoo) was reached on the 19th of April. From this position to the settled districts a route was found without difficulty—indeed, with great ease to Landsborough. On the 21st of May, being 103 days from the start, Williams's station, on the Warrego, was reached, where intelligence was first received regarding the fate of Burke and Wills. The remainder of the journey across the continent was made by the Darling River and Menindie to Melbourne. It proved of the highest value to the squatting interest, and led to the occupation of an immense extent of country for squatting purposes. After an experience of twenty years in Australia, Landsborough testified that the best land he had seen was in the district of Carpentaria.

CHAPTER XIV.

JOHN M'DOUALL STUART'S EXPEDITIONS IN THE SOUTH, TO THE CENTRE, AND ACROSS THE CONTINENT.

THE brave adventurer who is next to engage our attention must be placed in the front rank of explorers. John M'Douall Stuart was excelled by none, and equalled by few, in the special qualities which command success in the arduous enterprise to which he devoted his life. As a practical bushman he probably stands without a rival. From first to last he spent over twenty years in the exploration of Australia, during which time he was the leader of six expeditions, in all of which he made important discoveries, and never failed to bring home his men, who had put their lives in his keeping. He first served under a great master, Captain Sturt, whom he accompanied in the capacity of draughtsman to the expedition which started for the centre of Australia in 1844. His own responsible and eminently successful labours in the same field will be sketched in the sequel. It is not too much to claim for M'Douall Stuart the palm of martyrdom in the cause which lay so near his heart. It is true that after his work was done he was not left without honours, and also rewards, both in land and money, but by that time he had lost the capacity for enjoying any of these things. From his last journey he returned, or rather was carried, more dead than alive, racked with the pains of scurvy, contracted in the centre of the continent, which he was the first to discover. He subsequently rallied a little, but never recovered his health, and died in England in 1869.

I.

The first of Stuart's journeys was undertaken on the solicitation, and also at the expense, of his friend Mr. Wm. Finke, and had for its object the discovery of new pastoral country in the unknown territory to the west and north-west of Lake Torrens. On the 10th of June, 1858, Stuart started from Mount Eyre with only two men, a white man and a blackfellow, taking with him a small complement of horses and a too scanty allowance of provisions. The first section of the journey, which was rugged and sterile, lay to the west of Lake Torrens, whose surface was occasionally sighted. Water was found at moderate distances on this part of the route, but the rough and stony country proved a serious difficulty to the horses, which were imperfectly shod. This contingency had been strangely overlooked, and no shoes had been provided for the journey. The blackfellow, who was supposed to know this country intimately, soon got bewildered, and proved of no service for the purpose he was intended to forward. The leader, being thus thrown upon his own resources, was also greatly inconvenienced in shaping his course by the frequent and extraordinary illusions of the mirage of the desert. Referring to one of these perplexing occasions he says:—" I think we have now made the dip of the country toward the south, but the mirage is so powerful that little bushes appear like great gum-trees, which makes it very difficult to judge what is before us; it is almost as bad as travelling in the dark. I never saw it so bright or so continuous as it is now; one would think the whole country was under water." Failing to obtain the object of his search in the north-west, Stuart now directed his journey to the south and east, exploring the central region between Lake Torrens and Lake Gairdner. In this quarter some small patches of fairly good country were found, but the water, in the few places where it was met with, proved to be as bitter as the sea. The blackfellow now, thinking it time to shift for himself, took the way that pleased him best, leaving only the white man, Foster, to assist Stuart in the thick of his difficulties. Hope of a successful issue to their labours was now fast ebbing from the breasts of these indomitable adventurers. After journeying hither and thither for 1,000 miles, they had failed in the prime object of the expedition, their provisions were rapidly disappearing, and the horses were too footsore to travel an ordinary day's march. At this stage the monotony of the scene was broken by a high mountain coming into view, which Stuart named Mount Finke, and from the summit of which he ventured to hope for a better prospect, or, if not, to alter his course. "If I see nothing from the top of the mount to-morrow," said he, "I must turn down to Fowler's Bay for water for the horses. . . . As I could not remain quiet, I got on one of the lower spurs of Mount Finke to see what was before me. The prospect is gloomy in the extreme. I could see a long distance, but nothing met the eye but a dense scrub, as black and dismal as midnight." From this mount, accordingly, a straight course was steered to the sea-coast, during which every camping-place is marked on the map by the name of "desert." In the matter of provisions, they had for some time been reduced to one meal a day, and toward the close of the journey it was found that only two more remained to carry them a distance of 100 miles. In this dire extremity they were glad to feed on kangaroo mice, which, happily, were here to be found in great abundance. They are described as elegant little creatures, about four inches in length, of the shape of a kangaroo, with a tail terminating in a sort of brush. By means of this resource against starvation the explorers were enabled to cross the remaining stages of the desert, and so reached the habitations of civilized men.

II.

Mr. Stuart was the first explorer who reached the centre of Australia. The journey which led to this memorable achievement is worthy of detailed narration; but before entering upon this story it may be proper to say a few words on two preliminary essays in exploration, which, in some measure, opened the way to this much-desired result.

About six months after his return from his first expedition, this indefatigable explorer started on a new journey to examine the extensive territory lying to the north of Lake Torrens and the east of Lake Eyre. This country proved, in some respects, a surprise to Australian discovery. It turned out to be unusually well watered, being furrowed at moderate intervals by a series of creeks, some of which were entitled to the name of rivers. But its most astonishing feature consisted in the myriads of springs, in groups ranging from two or three to more than a dozen in number. Some of these sent forth a stream of water which might have turned a mill-wheel, and continued to run a mile from the source. From this circumstance the whole territory has, not inaptly, been called the "spring" country. Another dominant feature was seen in the extraordinary abundance of quartz reefs, many of which bore plain indications of being auriferous, but, of course, could not be fairly tested by any appliances which were then to hand. Towards the close of the same year (1859) another journey was made to this part of Australia, when more accurate surveys were obtained, and the boundaries of a number of squatting runs laid down. In both of these expeditions important service was rendered to the better knowledge of this country, but they were especially valuable as furnishing Stuart with an advanced starting-point for his heroic project of crossing the continent from south to north. This arduous, but happily successful, enterprise will now be described in its main outlines.

This expedition, which consisted of only three men and thirteen horses, set out on the 2nd of March, 1860, from Chambers's Creek, a valuable water supply which had been discovered by Stuart in 1858. For some time his course lay through an extensive tract of country which, though yet unoccupied, had become well known to this, its first explorer. Toward the northern part they followed the River Neale, which furnished plenty of water, and led them into the unknown country. The next important creeks to be discovered and crossed were the Hamilton, the Stephenson, and the Finke. After crossing the latter there began to heave into sight a strange and striking mountain structure, which presented the appearance of a locomotive engine with its funnel. " We proceeded," says the journal, "towards this remarkable pillar through heavy sand-hills covered with spinifex, and, at 12 miles from last night's camp, arrived at it. It is a pillar of sandstone, standing on a hill upwards of 100 feet high. From the base of the pillar to its top is about 150 feet, quite perpendicular, and it is 20 feet wide by 10 feet deep, with two small peaks on the top. I have named it Chambers's Pillar, in honour of James Chambers, Esq., who has been my great supporter in all my explorations." Much good country had been traversed before this point was reached; indeed, the whole of this route was a surprise in this respect, as it had been expected to land them in a great central desert. Instead of finding a barren wilderness, the continuation of the journey brought them into another splendid tract, watered by a creek named the Hugh, which, after being followed for a long distance, terminated in a high mountain-chain. To scale its rugged flanks and penetrate the dense thickets of mulga proved to be a most formidable task, their clothes and skin being torn in forcing a passage through the living and the dead timber. This range—the James—was succeeded by two other chains, which were named the Waterhouse and the M'Donnell Ranges, the latter of which have since become a well-known landmark in the history of more recent explorations. Stuart thus describes the view he obtained from the north gorge of these mountains:—" From the foot of this for about five miles is an open grassy country, with a few small patches of bushes. A number of gum-tree creeks come from the ranges and seem to empty themselves in the plains. The country in the ranges is as fine a pastoral hill-country as a man could wish to possess— grass to the top of the hills, and abundance of water through the whole of the ranges." Still heading northward, the expedition reached a position, on the 22nd of April, which is very memorable in the annals of Australia. The goal which had proved the incitement to so many sacrifices during a long period of our history was now reached at last. Mr. Stuart was standing in the centre of the continent. This achievement, of which he might well have been proud, is intimated by the following modest entry in his diary:—" To-day I find by my observation of the sun —111° 0′ 30″—that I am now camped in the centre of Australia. I have marked a tree and planted the British flag there. There is a high mount about two miles and a half to north-north-east. I wish it had been in the centre; but on it, to-morrow, I will raise a cone of stones and plant the flag there and name it Central Mount Stuart." This ceremony was performed on the day following, when a fine view was obtained from the summit of this high mountain. The aspect of the central region of Australia must have been a surprise to the first discoverer, for it falsified the prophecies of half a century. The centre of Australia was as much a matter of curiosity and conjecture in our early history as the North Pole is at the present time. Oxley was first in the field, with his pet theory of an inland sea. This conjecture received its quietus from Sturt, but it was only to make room for the opposite fallacy of a stony desert. Now, at last, when the veil was lifted and the reality disclosed, it turned out to be just that which nobody had prophesied and few had ventured to expect. It was simply a fine country, abounding in grass, and fairly supplied with water. Both now and afterwards it was used by Stuart as a recruiting-ground for his toil-worn expedition. Leaving part of his little force here for the present, the leader made a tentative effort to ascertain whether there was any practicable route out west to the Victoria River. Finding none, he returned, and kept steering his former course. As if the centre had been the natural goal of the journey, he met with nothing but difficulties in the attempt to penetrate further to the north. He himself had fallen a victim to scurvy, which was only slightly relieved by the native cucumber, his only resource. Water became even harder to find. The horses, also, which were too much of the cart breed, did not well stand a hard pinch. Above all, the blacks, who had never been friendly, became the more hostile the further the expedition advanced. The crisis was reached when they made an encampment on Attack Creek. Here the aborigines set fire to the grass, and tried every stratagem to separate the explorers from their horses, after which there would soon have been an end to the expedition. Failing in this device, they next mustered their forces and attacked the strangers in the proportion of ten to one. Even so, they had to come off second best for the time being. Nevertheless, Stuart deemed it scarcely prudent to oppose himself to a tribe of warlike blacks in the centre of Australia, with an army consisting of two men, all told, himself being commander-in-chief. Nothing further remained but to submit to the inevitable, which he accordingly did, and returned to the most northern settlements of South Australia.

III.

Mr. Stuart reached Adelaide in October, 1860. When it became known that he had encamped in the centre of Australia and pushed his way considerably further north, the public enthusiasm again rose to fever heat in the cause of exploration. The Parliament, which never failed in its duty in this business, again came forward with a vote of £2,500 to provide for another and a larger expedition, which was speedily organized, with the old and well-tried explorer for its leader. He took with him seven men, thirty horses, and thirty weeks' provisions. The former route was followed, with a little deviation, as far as Attack Creek, the scene of the previous repulse. In all his journeys Stuart had the shrewdness to search out and follow up mountain-systems, as being the physical conformation most likely to furnish the needful supply of water. Still on the look-out for this good fortune, Attack Creek had not been far left in the rear when an elevated chain—the Whittington Range—was discovered, and followed for a long distance. It led them on to Tomkinson's Creek, containing a large supply of water, which served as a base for immediate operations, and was afterwards turned to good account as a retreat in time of difficulty. Another mountain-system—named the Warburton—was met with in the next stage of the journey. Like the former, it was heading too much to the north to suit Stuart's intention of making for the Victoria River, on the western coast. Breaking away from the mountains, repeated attempts were made to find a route in the required direction. The high lands soon shaded away into an interminable, but very fertile champaign country, which received the name of Sturt's Plains, in honour of the "father of Australian exploration." But it proved to be absolutely arid, and blocked on all sides by impenetrable scrubs, varied only by low red sand-hills. Through these impervious scrubs, on the west, a passage would have to be forced, or the expedition must end in failure. The latter alternative was not to be thought of till every expedient had been exhausted. Leaving a portion of his force in the depôt, Stuart, three several times, started with a light party to pierce his way through the most forbidding obstacles he had ever experienced in his journeys. It was with the greatest difficulty the horses could be brought to face this formidable barrier; and when forced to do so, the animals were injured and the explorers' clothes torn to shreds. It was hard to persevere in the face of such sacrifices; yet it was done manfully enough, and might have been crowned with success but for the absolute failure of water. The furthest point reached in these assaults on the impervious west was only a hundred miles distant from Gregory's last camp on the Camfield; and if this short space could have been bridged over the final aim of the expedition would have been easily attained. To accomplish this object, Stuart did all that man could do in such a situation. Nothing could be more admirable than the pluck and perseverance displayed in this conflict with the impossible. But he, too, like all mortals, had to yield to stern necessity. With a heavy heart he turned his back on the coveted north-west and retreated to the old camping-ground on the Tomkinson. Even yet unwilling to leave any alternative untried, he now modified his plan, and proposed to strike north for the Gulf of Carpentaria, if such a course might be possible. This, unhappily, it proved not to be. His path was effectually barred in this direction also. After the most desperate effort nothing remained but to abandon the enterprise and return to the haunts of civilization. The following entry in his journal shows with how much regret this retreat was forced upon him:—" It certainly is a great disappointment to me not to be able to get through, but I believe I have left nothing untried that has been in my power. I have tried to make the Gulf and the river (Victoria) both before rain fell and immediately after it had fallen, but the results were the same —*unsuccessful*. I shall commence my homeward journey to-morrow morning. The horses have had a severe trial from the long journeys they have made, and the great hardships and privations they have undergone. On my last journey they were one hundred and six hours without water." So ended this second heroic effort to cross the continent. Notwithstanding his defeat, Stuart had succeeded in penetrating one hundred miles beyond the furthest point reached on the previous journey. His most advanced position was lat. 17° long. 133°.

IV.

Now, at last, we are to see the reward of perseverance. If Fortune has any favour for the brave, it was time to smile on John M'Douall Stuart. Two noble efforts had ended in failure, but this third attempt was to be crowned with complete success, and land the explorer on the much-coveted shores of the Indian Ocean. A month had not elapsed since his return from the second journey when the Government of South Australia despatched him on his third and final expedition. Being provided with reinforcements, he left the settled districts in January, 1862, and by the 8th of April had reached Newcastle Water, the most northern camping-ground of the former journey. Without loss of time he made a renewed attempt to pierce the north-western scrub and carve his way to the Victoria River. But again his Herculean struggles proved to be only wasted effort. This route was accordingly abandoned, finally and for ever, as being absolutely impracticable. The line of march was now directed to the north, with a view of cutting the track of Leichhardt's and Gregory's discoveries, and thus gaining the Roper River, which enters the Gulf of Carpentaria. This new project proved more easy in the accomplishment than he had ventured to expect. There were, of course, stubborn obstacles to be overcome; but water, the great requirement, was found at manageable intervals, bringing the party on, by a succession of ponds, first to the Daly Waters, and thence to an important river, which was named the Strangway. This bridge over the wilderness conducted them to the much-desired Roper River. It is described as a noble stream, draining a magnificent country, and exceeding in volume any the explorers had hitherto seen. This clue having been followed in the direction of its source, led the expedition a long way towards its destination on the shores of the Indian Ocean. After it failed them by turning too far to the north, only a short intervening tract had to be crossed before the Adelaide River, one of the known western streams, was reached. Again the route lay through some of the finest country in Australia, containing much that was new both in flora and fauna. The valley of this river was constantly revealing to the eyes of the strangers some botanical surprise — giant bamboos, fairy-like palms, and magnificent water-lilies on the placid bosom of its longer reaches. There was only one drawback, and that a rather serious one. It was the paradise of mosquitoes, which made a common prey of the intruders, allowing them no rest by night, and leaving mementos of their attachment that could not be forgotten during the day. But through pleasure and pain the expedition pushed on towards the attainment of its purpose. The leader so managed the last stage as to make the conclusion of the journey a surprise to his men. He knew the ocean to be near at hand, but kept the good news a secret till his party should be in a position to behold it with their own eyes. "At eight miles and a half," says he, "we came upon a broad valley of black alluvial soil, covered with long grass. From this I can hear the wash of the sea. On the other side of the valley, which is rather more than a quarter of a mile wide, is growing a line of thick heavy bushes, very dense, showing that to be the boundary of the beach. Crossed the valley and entered the scrub, which was a complete network of vines. Stopped the horses to clear a way, while I advanced a few yards on the beach, and was gratified and delighted to behold the waters of the Indian Ocean, in Van Diemen's Gulf, before the party with the horses knew anything of its proximity. Thring, who rode in advance of me, called out 'The sea!' which so took them all by surprise, and they were so astonished, that he had to repeat the call before they fully understood what was meant. They then immediately gave three long and hearty cheers. . . . . I dipped my feet and washed my hands, as I had promised the late Governor, Sir Richard M'Donnell, I would do if I reached it. Thus I have, through the instrumentality of Divine Providence, been led to accomplish the great object of the expedition, and to take the whole party safely as witnesses to the fact, and through one of the finest countries man could wish to behold. From Newcastle Water to the sea-beach the main body of the horses have been only one night without water, and then got it the next day." The Union Jack was now hoisted, and near the foot of a marked tree there was buried, in a tin, a paper containing the following inscription:—" The exploring party under the command of John M'Douall Stuart arrived at this spot on the 25th day of July, 1862, having crossed the entire continent of Australia, from the Southern to the Indian Ocean, passing through the centre. They left the city of Adelaide on the 26th day of October, 1861, and the most northern station of the colony on the 21st day of January, 1862. To commemorate this happy event they have raised this flag, bearing his name. All well. God save the Queen!" Burke and Wills had crossed the same continent to the Gulf of Carpentaria nearly eighteen months earlier, but this achievement in no way detracts from the merit of Stuart's success, for his journey was entirely independent of their, or any other, expedition. The felicitous termination of this splendid enterprise marks a principal era in the history of Australian exploration. It led directly to three important results—the annexation of the northern territory to South Australia, the establishment of a colonial settlement at Port Darwin, and the construction of the transcontinental telegraph along almost the whole route of this expedition.

CHAPTER XV.

COLONEL WARBURTON'S JOURNEY ACROSS THE WESTERN INTERIOR.

M'DOUALL STUART'S crowning feat in exploration was soon turned to good account. The idea of a transcontinental telegraph now passed from the realms of Utopia and became a realized fact. The commercial interests of Australia had been urgently in need of communication with the Indo-European lines already existing, but the great desert of the interior was believed to interpose an impenetrable barrier. Now, at last, this misconception, which had been founded on ignorance, was removed by Stuart, who discovered a belt of good country stretching across the interior and reaching to the Indian Ocean. Along this route, with few deviations, the line runs from the Adelaide extension in the south to Port Darwin in the north. In this most creditable enterprise, which was com- completed in 1872, South Australia spent £370,000, and rendered excellent service to the exploration, as well as to the commercial interests, of Australia. Here was a new base-line for explorers, intersecting the continent from end to end. This advantage was not long in being put to practical use. In South Australia the question of further exploration began to be agitated as soon as the line was opened. The Government was importuned for means to provide for an expedition to cut through the western interior, starting from the telegraph line at the centre of the continent. No aid was obtained from this quarter; nevertheless, the projected tour of discovery did not fall through, for two private gentlemen, the Hon. Thomas Elder and Mr. W. W. Hughes, now came forward and offered to bear the expense of the expedition. The next important step was the choice of a leader, who was happily found in Colonel P. E. Warburton. This brave man was born in Cheshire, England, in 1813. He was early trained for the military profession, and served in India from 1831 to 1853. About the latter date he came out to South Australia, where he was appointed Commissioner of Police, and subsequently held the position of Commandant of the volunteer forces till 1874. During these later years he had been engaged in several essays in exploration, in which he rendered good service to his country and prepared himself for the perilous, but successful, journey with which his name will ever be associated.

The proper starting-point for the expedition was fixed for Alice Springs, a station on the overland telegraph, situated almost in the centre of Australia; and it was the leader's intention to make for the city of Perth, in the west, by the most direct course that could be found—a purpose which came to be considerably modified under the pressure of a terrible necessity. The rendezvous, 1,120 miles distant from Adelaide, was reached by way of Beltana, along a route now beginning to be pretty well known, and all was prepared for the start by the 15th of April, 1873. The expedition, now first in the line of march, consisted of Colonel Warburton as leader, R. Warburton (his son), J. W. Lewis, D. White, two Afghans, and a black boy. The only beasts of burden were camels, which amounted to seventeen in number, and the supply of provisions was calculated to last for six months. The route for a short distance northward kept the line of the telegraph, till the Burt Creek was reached, after which it deflected toward the west. The difficulties which beset this journey began at the beginning and continued to its close, only increasing in severity with terrible consistency. Want of water compelled them again and again to retreat to former encampments, thus causing a great part of the route to be travelled over two or three times. From this cause the eastern boundary of South Australia had to be crossed three times before permanent progress could be made in the proper course. From first to last the country proved to be a barren waste, without creek or river affording a supply of water. In the earlier part of the journey an occasional oasis was met with containing permanent lakelets, at which the explorers would gladly have lingered to recruit themselves and rest the camels; but this delay meant consumption of the provisions, which it soon became evident were too scanty from the first. Warburton wisely resolved to feel his way as he proceeded through the desert by sending scouts in advance to search for water. This was seldom found, except in extremely sparse wells, which were used by the aborigines, and sometimes indicated by the smoke of their camps, but in hardly a single instance was direct information obtained from the blacks. The native wells in the sand not unusually indicated, rather than contained, water, and had often to be excavated to much greater depth. In this way, for the most part, was the desert crossed. When water was announced, an advance was made one stage further and a search party again sent out. It often happened that no water could be found by the scouts after the most exhausting search, further progress being thus rendered impossible. In these cases there was no help for it but to change the direction, as far as their object would permit, and seek another tentative route. This was indescribably trying to their spirits, but the other alternative was to perish in the sand. On some few occasions the clouds came to their relief and burst in thunderstorms. Even when only a slight shower fell, a few buckets of water were secured by spreading a tarpaulin on the ground. On the 9th of May a deep glen was found in a range of hills. Here was an excellent supply of water, shaded by basalt rocks, rising to the height of 300 ft. Here, too, the weary wanderers rested for a few days, as also at Waterloo Wells, a little ahead, for which they had to pay a penalty in the permanent loss of four camels, which suddenly decamped. They were tracked for a hundred miles, but never recovered.

Hitherto their progress had been slow and discouraging. They had travelled 1,700 miles, but were yet at no great distance from Alice Springs. Nor was the outlook any more encouraging. Day after day it was the same weary journeying over spinifex ridges and sandy valleys, without any indication of the fine country they had hoped to discover; but, to their credit be it said, no one even hinted about giving up the enterprise. By the 17th of August a notable stage in their progress was reached. Warburton ascertained that he could not be more than ten miles distant from the most southern point reached by Mr. A. C. Gregory in 1856. The Colonel ascended a neighbouring hill to see if he could catch a glimpse of Termination Lake, into which Sturt's Creek had been found to empty itself. This salt lake was concealed by a range of sand-hills; but Warburton verified his position, and thus had virtually connected his own survey from the centre with the Gregory discoveries in the north. Advancing slowly, but surely, towards the west, a fine freshwater lake was discovered on the 30th. It abounded in waterfowl, which were more easily shot than recovered, as they had no means of reaching them in the water. From this point onward their troubles began to thicken with ominous rapidity. Eight of the seventeen camels were gone, while the stock of provisions, too, began to appear uncomfortably small, and had to be dealt out with a niggardly hand. It now became evident to the Colonel that the original plan of proceeding to Perth was impracticable, and he resolved to head further to the north, so as to strike the Oakover River and save the expedition. Their troubles were truly most afflicting in this great and terrible wilderness. The heat and toil of travelling wore them out by day, and myriads of black ants deprived them of their sleep at night. They were now living on camels' flesh, dried in the sun, the only sauce being an occasional bird which fell to their guns. By the 2nd of November they had been reduced to dire extremity, both of famine and thirst. The Oakover was estimated to be about 150 miles distant, and it was resolved to make a rush for it, taking their chance of an accidental discovery of water to keep them in life, for it was now a question of mere life and death. Respecting this latter and awfully perilous stage of the journey, it will be better to let Colonel Warburton speak for himself. The following extracts are from the entries in his journal as made during the crisis of his sufferings, when hope was fast giving place to despair:—"We killed our last meat on the 20th October; a large bull camel has, therefore, fed us for three weeks. It must be remembered that we have had no flour, tea, or sugar, neither have we an atom of salt, so we cannot salt our meat. We are seven in all, and are living entirely upon sundried slips of meat which are as tasteless and innutritious as a piece of dead bark. . . . We have abandoned everything but our small supply of water and meat, and each party has a gun. . . We are hemmed in on every side: every trial we make fails; and I can now only hope that some one or more of the party may reach water sooner or later. As for myself, I can see no hope of life, for I cannot hold up without food and water. I have given Lewis written instructions to justify his leaving me, should I die, and have made such arrangements as I can for the preservation of my journal and maps. . . . My party, at least, are now in that state that, unless it please God to save us, we cannot live more than 24 hours. We are at our last drop of water, and the smallest bit of dried meat chokes me. I fear my son must share my fate, as he refuses to leave me. God have mercy upon us, for we are brought very low, and by the time death reaches us we shall not regret exchanging our present misery for that state in which the weary are at rest. We have tried to do our duty, and have been disappointed in all our expectations. I have been in excellent health during the whole journey, and am so still, being merely worn out from want of food and water. Let no self-reproaches afflict any respecting me. I undertook this journey for the benefit of my family, and I was quite equal to it under all the circumstances that could be reasonably anticipated, but difficulties and losses have come upon us so thickly for the last few months that we have not been able to move. Thus, our provisions are gone; but this would not have stopped us could we have found water without such laborious search. The country is terrible. I do not believe men ever traversed so vast an extent of continuous desert." They were, indeed, brought to the last extreme of misery. But man's extremity is God's opportunity. A search party found a good well about twelve miles distant, which supplied all their necessities, and saved their lives. Another fortnight brought the forlorn wanderers to a creek with a good store of water at intervals. This proved to be a tributary of the Oakover, to the banks of which they were thus led by such stages as could be travelled in their deplorably emaciated condition. The outskirts of civilization were all but reached. The pastoral station of De Grey was believed to be only a few days' travelling down the river, and a small detachment was sent to implore succour. The distance was really 170 miles, and three weary weeks had to be spent in hoping against hope till relief arrived. Help did come in abundance, and as speedily as was possible in the circumstances. The toils of the wilderness wanderings were now over; all that remained was a terrible retrospect. It was reckoned they had not travelled less than 4,000 miles, including deviations and retreats when further advance became impracticable through want of water. The result, looked at from an explorer's point of view, was, of course, a flat disappointment. Some had confidently expected to hear of a good pastoral country being discovered in the western interior which would prove a new home to the enterprising squatter, and be depastured by myriads of flocks and herds. Instead of this wished-for discovery, Colonel Warburton had to follow in the wake of Captain Sturt, and tell yet another tale of an arid desert with dreary ridges of sand succeeding each other like the waves of the sea —a country of no use to civilized, and very little to savage, man. Yet, even so, a good service had been rendered to the knowledge of Australian geography. Where the truth has to be known it is something even to reach a negative result. If the western interior is a desert, it is a real gain to have this fact ascertained and placed on record. Another question set at rest by this expedition is the incomparable superiority of camels in Australian exploration, in point of endurance and in making long stages without water. A horse requires to be watered every twelve hours, but a camel will go without it for ten or twelve days on a pinch. This was not the first time they had been tried in Australia. Burke and Wills started with more "ships of the desert" than Warburton; but the mismanagement which involved that enterprise in fatal disaster deprived the experiment of a fair chance of success. Warburton's was pre-eminently the camel expedition of Australia. The result justified the means. With all the aid of these invaluable beasts of burden the expedition, indeed, was brought to the very brink of ruin; but without them everyone must inevitably have perished.

CHAPTER XVI.

THE HON. JOHN FORREST'S EXPLORATIONS IN WESTERN AUSTRALIA.

This distinguished explorer is a native of West Australia, and an honour to his country. He is a man of ability, well educated, and thoroughly competent for the work to which he has devoted so much of his time and attention. In early life he entered the Survey Department, where his services were appreciated and rewarded by an appointment, in 1876, to the office of Deputy Surveyor-General. Mr. Forrest has gained imperishable laurels in the field of exploration. His services in the three following expeditions entitle him to a high position among the Australian explorers. A short notice of each is all that our space permits.

I.

About the close of 1868 a report reached Perth to the effect that natives in the eastern districts knew of a party of white men who had been murdered some twenty years earlier. This rumour was strongly confirmed by a gentleman who had penetrated into the interior in search of sheep-runs. He reported that his native guide had assured him he had been to the very spot where the murder had been committed, and had seen the remains of white men. His story was very circumstantial, stating that it was on the border of a large lake, and that the white men were killed while making damper. He volunteered, moreover, to conduct any party to the scene of the murder. The story possessed a sufficient likeness to truth to impose on grave and sober-minded men. Among these was Baron Von Mueller, of Melbourne, who organized a party to proceed to the spot, in the hope of finding the remains of Leichhardt's expedition. He intended to take the lead himself, but this purpose he had to change, through business engagements, and the expedition accordingly was placed under the command of Mr. John Forrest. The route lay to the north-east from Perth. The party was able to penetrate 250 miles in advance of former expeditions. This was, so far, another gain to the knowledge of Australian geography; but the new country was found to be unsuitable for pastoral or agricultural purposes. In regard to its principal object, the expedition turned out a complete failure, adding only one other proof of the utter worthlessness of aboriginal testimony. The blackfellow who had led them out with such confidence made some significant admissions as they proceeded on the journey. First, he had not, properly speaking, been at the place himself, or seen the relics, but had heard of them from others of the black fraternity; then, again, he could not be sure whether they were the bones of men or horses—more likely, perhaps, the latter. Finally, it was pretty clearly ascertained that the whole story had originated from the remains of a number of horses which had belonged to the explorer Austin, and were poisoned in that neighbourhood. No traces of Leichhardt were found in that quarter, nor is it at all probable that he had penetrated so far west.

II.

Almost immediately after returning from the search after Leichhardt, Mr. Forrest was put in command of a second expedition. Governor Weld was anxious to obtain a more accurate survey of the southern coast between Perth and Adelaide, with a view to telegraphic connection. The largest and most difficult part of the route lay along the Great Australian Bight, which had been traversed with terrible suffering by Mr. E. J. Eyre thirty years previously. Since that time a little more information had been gained, tending to lessen the horrors of travel in that forbidding region; and Port Eucla, a valuable harbour, had been discovered just within the eastern boundary of West Australia. But the whole of the southern country from Perth to Adelaide required to be examined afresh for the object which was now contemplated. Mr. John Forrest was easily persuaded to lead this expedition, which consisted of his brother, Mr. Alexander Forrest, as second in command, Police Constable M'Larty, a farrier, and two aboriginals. A small schooner, the *Adur*, was despatched, to wait with supplies at Esperance Bay, Israelite Bay, and Port Eucla—an arrangement which greatly lessened the difficulties and dangers of the expedition. After reaching the Great Bight the party followed, in a reverse direction, the line of Eyre's journey, keeping a little more inland, though they were never more than thirty miles from the sea. So far as the old explorer's tracks were followed, Forrest had the advantage of finding an occasional supply of water as indicated on the chart, and when he deviated from this route he was well rewarded by the discovery of better, and sometimes of really first-class country. The season, though too dry, seems to have been less so than when Eyre encountered the perils of this region, and for this reason occasional surface water was found, in very limited quantities. Yet on several of the long waterless stages both men and horses were near their last gasp in the agonies of thirst. From Port Eucla an attempt was made to penetrate for some distance to the north, in the interest of discovery. The land appeared, and has since been proved, to be of the best quality, but absolute want of water compelled the explorers to beat a retreat when they had proceeded only about thirty miles inland. The expedition again started on its proper course and rounded the head of the Bight. Soon an escort was in readiness from South Australia, which led them through the Gawler Ranges to the city of Adelaide. The party had started on the 30th of March, 1870, and their destination was reached on the 27th of August—not half the time Mr. Eyre had required for a much shorter journey. This new adventure in exploration was highly successful. A practicable route for the telegraph having been found, the line was constructed in the course of another year or two, thus connecting Perth with the intercolonial and also with the European telegraphic systems. Fine reaches of the best pastoral country were examined or indicated lying to the north of the wretched seaboard, the only drawback being the absence of permanent water. This difficulty is now being overcome by boring, by which means an ample supply is obtained at a reasonable depth. The latest proposal is to run a railway from Perth to Port Eucla, with probable extension to Adelaide. A syndicate has offered to construct it on the land-grant system, engineers are presently engaged on the survey, and its completion may be accepted as one of the great events of the near future.

III.

Mr. John Forrest's third expedition was much more arduous, as it was also of greater geographical importance, than either of the preceding. Before the transcontinental telegraph was fully completed, he proposed to the authorities at Perth to lead an exploring party across the centre of Western Australia from Champion Bay to the route of the new line, on condition of a grant from the Treasury of £400 for expenses, himself engaging to provide another £200. The proposal was gladly accepted, and no time was lost in making the necessary preparations. His party, as finally organized, consisted of Alexander Forrest, five whites, two aboriginals, and twenty-one horses. It being resolved to keep the line of the Murchison to its sources, the start was made from Geraldton, Champion Bay, on the 1st of April, 1874. For some time the course lay to the south of the river, which was not joined till the 23rd, after which beautifully grassed country was travelled over. The Murchison in its upper waters divided into several channels, causing some perplexity. One of these was selected, and followed as far as it served their purpose, and then the course was directed to the watershed. Now they found themselves in a dry, barren land, which afforded the scantiest supply of water, and only after laborious search—sometimes not even then. Occasionally, but only at long intervals, a good native well was reached, when the temptation to rest for several days was irresistible. To the most noted of these Mr. Forrest gave the name of the Weld Springs, in honour of the Governor, who ever did his utmost to forward the exploration of the interior. The encampment at Weld Springs was not an unbroken pleasure. The blacks were numerous in the neighbourhood, and irreconcilably hostile. Finding his party assailed with murderous intent, Forrest, seeing it had become a question of self-defence, fired upon the natives, and some blood was shed. But for this act of stern necessity, it is evident that the explorers must have perished. This pleasant spot was but an oasis in a great desert, which became the more inhospitable the further they penetrated into its secrets. For 600 miles they had to thread their way through a wilderness of spinifex, sometimes also approaching the verge of despair through want of water, in search of which the scouts had always to scour the country. In this desert the natives were seldom seen, and still more rarely could they be induced to come within speaking distance. At one place they decamped on the first appearance of the intruders on their desert home, leaving a whole kangaroo roasting on the fire. This would have been quite a godsend for Warburton and his party, but happily the present expedition was never reduced to such dire necessity. In another respect, too, Forrest seems to have had better luck than his brother explorers. During the latter part of his journey a kind of fig-tree *(Ficus platypoda)* was occasionally met with, producing an agreeable fruit about the size of a bullet. Such a discovery in the wilds of Australia is nothing short of a marvel. Nature has reserved few such favours for this country. Yet still better fortune was at hand. It became evident, first by faint and then by very plain indications, that they were coming on the tracks of Europeans. Only a short time previously Mr. Giles and Mr. Gosse had separately been out in these parts, but had to return for want of water. Still, a marked tree or an old camping-ground was an inspiring object, seeing they had been made by travellers who had started from the opposite end of the journey. Much yet remained to be done, but the ground was now got over with much better heart. The monotony of the desert-wandering had been much relieved in a manner highly creditable to Mr. Forrest. Here, as in all his explorations, he remembered the Sabbath day to keep it holy. Regularly, as the Sunday came round, divine service was read in the camp. Even the old habit of a good Sunday dinner was not forgotten. People in different circumstances might not have thought the cheer much to be envied; but hunger is the best sauce. If a pigeon or a parrot could be secured at the seasonable time it was reserved as a special treat for the Sunday dinner. But better things were in store. Perseverance had not much longer to wait for its reward. Following the tracks of the preceding explorers, they came on to the Marryat River, which led them on to the Alberga, and this clue finally conducted the weary wanderers to the long-desired telegraph line. The journal of the expedition contains the following entry for the 27th August, 1874:—"Continued east for about twelve miles, and then E.N.E. for three miles, and reached the telegraph line between Adelaide and Port Darwin, and camped." [The 104th camp from the start.] "Long and continued cheers came from our little band as they beheld at last the goal to which we have been travelling for so long. I felt rejoiced and relieved from anxiety; and in reflecting on the long time of travel we had performed through an unknown country, almost a wilderness, felt very thankful to that good Providence that had guarded and guided us so safely through it." A well-beaten track had now been made along the telegraph line, which the party followed, proceeding to the south. In a day or two the Peak station was reached. From this point the journey to Adelaide was made by easy stages. Forrest's track lay a long way south of Warburton's, and threw a streak of light across another dark region of the western half of Australia. The results of the journey are thus summed up in the explorer's own words:—"The whole of the country, from the settled districts near Champion Bay to the head of the Murchison, is admirably suited for pastoral settlement, and in a very short time will be taken up and stocked; indeed, some has already been occupied. From the head of the Murchison to the 129th meridian, the boundary of our colony, I do not think will ever be settled. Of course, there are many grassy patches, such as at Windich Springs, the Weld Springs, all round Mount Moore, and other places; but they are so isolated, and of such extent, that it would never pay to take stock to them. The general character of this immense tract is a gently undulating spinifex desert—*Festuca (Triodia) irritans*, the spinifex of the desert explorers, but not the spinifex of science. It is lightly wooded . . . . and there is a great absence of any large timber."

CHAPTER XVII.

MR. ERNEST GILES'S EXPLORATIONS IN CENTRAL AND WESTERN AUSTRALIA.

MR. ERNEST GILES is a native of Bristol, in England. As soon as his education was finished he rejoined his father and family, who had preceded him to Australia. He very early developed a passion for exploration, and gained valuable experience in connection with various expeditions which he served in a subordinate capacity. His own fame as an explorer rests securely on the following enterprises :—

I.

Shortly after the construction of the Port Darwin telegraph, Mr. Giles made a persevering attempt to lead a small party from Chambers's Pillar to the sources of the Murchison River. The expenses were provided partly by himself and partly by Baron Von Mueller, of Melbourne. The party consisted of Messrs. Giles, Carmichael, and A. Robinson, with fifteen horses and one dog. The start was made about the middle of August, 1872. For the early part of the journey the River Finke was followed, but it led them into a rugged, mountainous country, in which travelling was difficult. The scenery was often charming, as one glen after another was explored.

Palm-Tree Glen, in particular, called forth unceasing admiration on account of the multitude of wild flowers which were "born to blush unseen and waste their sweetness on the desert air." "I collected to-day," says Mr. Giles, "and during the other days since we have been in this glen, a number of most beautiful flowers, which grow in profusion in this otherwise desolate glen. I am literally surrounded by fair flowers of many a changing hue. Why Nature should scatter such floral gems in such a sterile region is difficult to understand; but such a variety of lovely flowers of every colour and perfume I have never met with previously. They alone would have induced me to name this the Glen of Flowers, but having found in it also so many of the stately palm-trees, I have called it the Glen of Palms." During a further advance among the outlying spurs of the M'Donnell Ranges, the Finke was left, or lost, and laborious search had often to be made for water. The mountains were high, but no creek was found with a longer course than twelve miles. The peaks often assumed strange and fantastic shapes, as the explorers have indicated by such names as Mount Peculiar, Haast's Bluff, &c. The following quotation from the journal shows how they were straitened at this time through want of water. After finding a little in the hollow of a rock, just sufficient to save life, Mr. Giles says:—"It was necessary to try to discover more water if possible, so, after breakfast, I walked away, but, after travelling up gullies and gorges, hills and valleys, I had to return quite unsuccessful, and I can only conclude that this water was permitted by a kind Providence to remain here in this lovely spot for my especial benefit. . . . I have, in gratitude, called it Mount Udor, as being the only one in this region where a drop of that requisite element was to be obtained. And when I left the udor had departed also." This incident occurred at the twenty-first camp from Chambers's Pillar. From this point a persevering, but unsuccessful, effort was made to strike out west in the direction of a chain named Ehrenberg's Mountain. Want of water again forced the party back on Mount Udor. A more southerly route led to the important discovery of a great saltwater lake, which was called Amadeus, after the then King of Spain, son of Victor Emanuel. Beyond this long, but comparatively narrow, sheet of water, a conspicuous mountain, named Olga, specially attracted the attention of Mr. Giles, who was anxious to reach it by rounding the lake. But this labour was prevented by an incident which, unhappily, caused the purpose of the expedition to collapse. Robinson had been seized with home-sickness, and the infection reached Carmichael, who obstinately refused to proceed any further. Giles tried the effect of moral suasion, which was the only weapon available for a volunteer. He pleaded the large supply of provisions, the importance of the enterprise, and the ignominy of turning back. But it was to no purpose. Carmichael had made up his mind and would listen to no arguments. Giles was now compelled to direct his march back to the telegraph line, "a baffled and beaten man." During this inglorious retreat the course lay by the Peterman, the Palmer, and the Finke rivers, and by this route the original camp No. 1 was reached. Here is the conclusion of the whole matter in Mr. Giles's own words:—" My expedition was over. I had failed in my object (to penetrate to the sources of the Murchison River) certainly, but not through any fault of mine, as I think any impartial reader of my journal will admit. . . . We travelled to the eastward along the course of the River Finke (homeward), and passed a few miles to the south of Chambers's Pillar, which had been my starting-point. I had left it but twelve weeks and four days to the time I re-sighted it, and during that interval I had traversed and laid down about a thousand miles of country. My expedition thus early ends. Had I been fortunate enough to have fallen upon a good, or even fair, line of country, the distance I actually travelled would have taken me across the continent."

II.

A second attempt was made by the same explorer shortly after his return from the first. The funds being provided by the liberality of the Victorian colonists, a light party, consisting of Messrs. Giles, Tietkens, Gibson, and Andrews, with twenty-four horses, were despatched for the purpose of crossing the western half of Australia. They left the telegraph road at the junction of the Stevenson and Alberga creeks on the 4th of August, 1873. The latter was followed for some distance westward, after which, by a short cross-country route to the north, the Hamilton River was reached, and taken as a guide so far as was practicable. This journey led to the discovery of four remarkable mountain-chains. The first of these was named Anthony Range. From one of the summits they beheld a sea of mountains, countless in number, many of which presented the most comically fantastic shapes and forms which the imagination can conceive. Ayer's Range was next reached, and an equally commanding view obtained from one of its heights. The next was the Musgrave Range, occupying a central position in a far-reaching expanse of good country. Here the natives were encountered in a hostile attitude, but were beaten off by the superior arms of four white men. After a journey of 400 miles they reached Mt. Olga, which had been sighted on the former expedition. In this neighbourhood also, they found the tracks of Mr. Gosse, a contemporary explorer, which led to a deviation from the proposed route. In Cavanagh's Range a depôt was established, as a basis for tentative explorations in a forbidding tract of country. About 110 miles from this centre they made a welcome discovery of a waterfall of 150 feet, sending forth a musical roar as it fell, and scattering around a plentiful shower of spray. This gladdening apparition in the desert received the name of the Alice Falls. The country in the immediate neighbourhood was also well grassed. This place has doubtless a future in store for it. Turning more to the north, in the direction of a broken country, another splendid range, named the Rawlinson, was discovered. It extended to 60 miles in length, with a breadth of five or six. The peaks were remarkably pointed and jagged. From this position an attempt was made to strike out in a north-westerly direction, but bad fortune compelled them to return after Mt. Destruction had been reached. Four of the horses had been lost in a journey of ninety miles; water was not to be found; the natives were troublesome; and the eye could discern nothing ahead but spinifex desert and rolling sand-hills. A return to the Rawlinson Range was, therefore, imperative. Having again rested for a little, another determined effort was made to force a passage due west across the interior and strike the outposts of settlement in Western Australia. All was done that man could do, but impossibilities are not to be accomplished. The western flanks of the Rawlinson Range faded away into a barren and waterless desert. Giles and Gibson had, as a gigantic effort of perseverance, penetrated 98 miles into this inhospitable waste. But no further could they go. Here, on the 23rd of April, the utmost bourne of the expedition was reached. One of the two horses here knocked up and died. This was the last time Gibson was seen. Giles did his utmost to bring him help, but he was never found. His bones lie somewhere in that awful wilderness, which to this day bears his name. When the furthest point was reached better fortune seemed to loom in the distance. Another range of lofty mountains was descried athwart the western horizon, which he called the Alfred and Marie, after the Duke and Duchess of Edinburgh. They might as well have been in the moon so far as Mr. Giles was concerned in his now pitiable plight. His own reflections were deplorably bitter:— "The hills bounding the western horizon were between thirty and forty miles away, and it was with extreme regret that I was compelled to relinquish a further attempt to reach them. Oh, how ardently I longed for a camel; how ardently I gazed upon the scene! At this moment I would even my jewel eternal have sold for power to span that gulf that lay between. But it could not be; situated as I was, I was compelled to retreat, and the sooner the better." Such was his destiny. After almost twelve months' wanderings in the wilderness, three of the four explorers escaped with their lives, and reached the central telegraph line on the 13th of July.

III.

Such battling with relentless fortune would have extinguished the spirit of adventure in most men. In the case of Mr. Giles it fanned it into a brighter flame. Refusing to be baffled, his noble perseverance was at length rewarded with a double journey across the western half of the continent. This expedition was fitted out by Sir Thomas Elder, of Adelaide, who supplied him with nineteen camels and provisions for eighteen months. The party consisted of Messrs. Giles, Tietkens, Young, A. Ross, P. Nicholls, Selah (an Afghan), and a black boy. The route proposed was from Youldah to Perth, and the start was made on the 27th July, 1875. This, though a successful, was a very trying journey. They crossed desert after desert for a distance of 1,500 miles. On one occasion they were reduced to the last extremity of thirst, and saved from perishing by the happy discovery of a spring in the Great Victoria Desert, 600 miles from the out-settlements of Western Australia. They reached Perth on the 10th November, having travelled a distance of 2,575 miles in about five months. The following is Mr. Giles's summary of the journey:—"The expedition has been successful, yet the country traversed for more than a thousand miles in a straight line was simply an undulating bed of dense scrub, except between the 125th and 127th meridians, the latitude being nearly the 30th parallel. Here an arm of the Great Southern Plain ran up and crossed our track, which, though grassy, was quite waterless. The waters were, indeed, few and far between throughout. On one occasion, a stretch of desert was encountered in which no water was obtainable for 325 miles, which only the marvellous sustaining powers of Mr. Elder's all-enduring beasts enabled us to cross. The next desert was only 180 miles to a mass of granite, where I saw natives for the first time on the expedition. They attacked us there, but we managed to drive them off. Mount Churchman was now only 160 miles distant, and we found water again before reaching it. We struck in at Toora, an out-station, where the shepherd was very hospitable. At other homesteads we were most kindly welcomed." By another journey, in a reverse direction, across the western interior, Mr. Giles returned to the central telegraph, which for so long had formed his base of operations. Leaving Perth on the 13th of January, 1876, he pushed north, and struck the Ashburton River, thence passed through 150 miles of desert, and from the opposite side reached the Alfred and Marie Range, from which he had been so piteously thrust back in 1873. He soon after reached the Rawlinson Range, which he had discovered on that same expedition. Being now in a known country, he passed safely through it, and reached the Peak telegraph station on the 23rd of August, 1876. His journey thence to Adelaide was ordinary travel in the Australian bush.

CHAPTER XVIII.

OTHER EXPLORERS IN WESTERN AUSTRALIA.— CONCLUSION.

THERE still remain a considerable number of the explorers of Western Australia, whose achievements, though inferior to the foregoing, would have called for particular notice had this been an exhaustive work. A very brief outline of the journeys of the most prominent is all that can be attempted here. We shall begin with Captain, afterwards Sir George, Grey, so well known in later times as a new Zealand statesman. From 1837 to 1840 he was occupied with two expeditions for the exploration of the country lying between the coast and the first range. Both journeys were exceedingly hazardous—none more so in this department of history. During the first Prince Regent's River was explored; but the most important result was the discovery of the River Glenelg, which was described as one of the finest in Australia. The second expedition was directed to Shark's Bay, which was reached in February, 1839. The most important discovery during this journey was the River Gascoyne. The expedition was soon overtaken by terrible misfortunes, which compelled the party to make for Swan River by the quickest route. The first attempt was made in a small boat, which got no further than Ganthcaume Bay, where it was dashed to pieces on the beach. To save their lives they had now to walk on foot along an inhospitable coast for 300 miles, with no more provisions than twenty pounds of flour and one pound of pork to each man. Grey struggled along and gave a heroic example to the men under his charge. When he arrived at Perth he looked like a spectre, and his most intimate friends did not know him. He has himself told us what was the secret of his moral strength :—" It may be asked," he said, " if, during such a trying period, I did not seek from religion that consolation which it is sure to afford. My answer is, yes; and I further feel assured that but for the support I derived from prayer and frequent perusal of the Scriptures, I should never have been able to have borne myself in such a manner as to have maintained discipline and confidence among the rest of the party; nor in my sufferings did I ever lose the consolation derived from a firm reliance upon the goodness of Providence. It is only those who go forth into perils and dangers, amidst which human foresight and strength can but little avail, and who find themselves day after day protected by an unseen influence, and ever and anon snatched from the very jaws of destruction by a power which is not of this world, who can at all estimate the knowledge of one's own weakness and littleness, and the firm reliance and trust upon the goodness of the Creator which the human heart is capable of feeling."

The next in order is Mr. J. S. Roe, Surveyor-

CONCLUSION.

General of Western Australia. With a party of six men, eleven horses, and four months' provisions, he started from York in September, 1848, for the southern part of the colony. Leaving the last stations of the River Avon, he went S. ½ S. in a direction which had not yet been explored. In a short time he got into a poor country, which contained the heads of the Avon, the Williams, the Arthur, and other rivers. In 45 miles further he came to the Pallinup River, the last water which had been crossed by Eyre on his journey along the Great Bight. He followed it to the neighbourhood of Cape Riche, the latter part of this stage being through a well-grassed country. Here a squatting station was found, and a much-needed rest obtained. The next effort was to make the Bremer Range. In the intervening part, a river, the Jeeramungup, was discovered in a good tract of country, which was again succeeded by poor land. The Bremer Range was reached by the 3rd November. There was a hard journey thence to the Russell Range, which was near Eyre's country, and of the same description. The coast was reached opposite the Recherche Archipelago. Roe had now travelled 1,000 miles from Swan River, and found it necessary to return, and in doing so kept very much to Eyre's track as far as Cape Riche. The most important result of this journey was the discovery of several seams of coal. The return to Perth was made by way of the Pallinup River. The party had been absent 149 days, and travelled 1,800 miles.

The third explorer who shall be briefly noticed is Mr. R. Austin, who was Assistant Surveyor-General. He was despatched by the Government to search for gold in the country north and east of the settled districts. The party consisted of ten men, twenty-seven horses, and 120 days' provisions. By the 10th of July, 1854, they had left the head of Swan River, and entered on a wretchedly poor country, in which all the bushes were dead. Another fifty miles' travel brought them to a table-land with some high mountains, the most conspicuous of which received the name of Mt. Kenneth. Soon after a severe mishap befell the expedition. The horses having eaten a poisonous plant, twenty-four died within a few hours, leaving the explorers in a very helpless condition. They pushed on, nevertheless, and displayed an admirable perseverance. On the 24th of August they reached a magnetic hill, which was called Mt. Magnet, and returned for rest to Recruit Flat. The country next traversed lay between the Great Salt Lake and West Mt. Magnet, dry, rough, and stony throughout. One curious discovery was a cave with life-like figures of animals drawn by the aborigines. Some similar exhibitions of savage art had previously been discovered by other explorers in the north and west. The party came again to poisonous bushes, and the horses had to be watched night and day. Thence, taking a westward course, they got within fifty miles of Shark's Bay, when want of food compelled them to retreat to the Geraldine mines on the Murchison

River. Here the party broke up, some returning to Perth by sea and the rest overland. The expedition failed in its principal object; nor was it in other respects much of a success.

It would be unpardonable to close this list without mention of Mr. F. T. Gregory's services in the exploration of West Australia. In April, 1858, he led an expedition from the Geraldine mines to examine the country between the Gascoyne River and Mt. Murchison. This effort was attended with much success. At least a million acres of good land were discovered —quite a Godsend for this colony, which is so rich in deserts. The principal places discovered and named were Mt. Nairn, Lockyer Range, Lyons River, the Alma, and Mt. Hall.

It is but right to add that the exploration of the interior has been largely indebted to private enterprise, of which there is no particular record. The pioneer squatters, in search of "fresh fields and pastures new," have not been afraid to invade unknown territories, nor have they gone without their reward. When a fine patch of country has been discovered they have usually been quite willing to sacrifice their merit as explorers to the caresses of private fortune, being mindful, perhaps, of the old proverb which tells us "the crow would have more to eat if he were less noisy over his food." The same cause has been helped on, also, by the search for gold, than which nothing will entice man further from home, or collect them in greater crowds. In this way much available country has lately been opened up in the Kimberley district of Western Australia, and the process is still going on, with many promising prospects. It is extremely probable that this northern region will soon be reckoned one of that colony's most valuable possessions, both in the squatting and the mining interests.

As the combined result of all the foregoing agencies, Australia has virtually ceased to be an unknown land by the close of the first century of our history. Even the great desert of Western Australia, real or supposed, has been crossed again and again, while lesser enterprises, issuing from all sides, have carried the fringe of the known territory further and further inland. Even yet the spirit of exploration keeps awake, and refuses to rest so long as a patch of the interior remains to be examined. While these sheets are passing through the press an exploring party, supported again by Adelaide, are preparing for the interior, in order to wrest from its grasp such secrets as it may yet retain.

It is pleasing to observe how a better acquaintance with Australia, both in the way of discovery and settlement, is surely leading on to the belief that it will yet be the home of a numerous population. For a long period it was reckoned unfit to be the habitation of civilized man, except along the seaboards. The want of water, and continuous deserts, were supposed to have placed the interior beyond the pale of settlement. But experience has already revealed a system of compensations by which this hasty judgment has come to be reversed, and the back country settled by a thriving population. There are deserts, indeed, in which one might search in vain for a blade of grass, but they contain many patches of nutritious shrubs, which not only keep alive, but even fatten, stock. Water, too, is scarce, but, by another of these admirable compensations, it is capable of being stored in any quantity, and for any length of time, without becoming putrid—an advantage unknown to the home countries. The rainfall, moreover, is very scant —perhaps not more than seven inches per annum in the far interior—but then the recent borings with the diamond drill have shown that an abundant supply may be obtained from subterranean sources. The latest announcement made to us, now standing on the threshold of the centennial year, is the most encouraging of all. By the ticking of the telegraph we learn that an experiment at Barcaldine, in Queensland, has brought to the surface of the bore a daily discharge of something approaching to 100,000 gallons of water fit for all purposes. Experience is ever revealing new relations of material adaptability. There is a sympathy between a country and its inhabitants, which may have a deeper foundation than the fancy of the poet. The land and the people are the complements of one another. "God made the earth to be inhabited," and there is now no fear of Australia being an exception to the rule.

INDEX.

Aborigines, 67, 79, 88, 103, 106, 123, 125, 127, 128, 136, 140, 147, 149, 150, 162, 179, 186, 191
Abundance, Mt., 160, 161
Adelaide, 97
    River, 23, 207
Albany, Port, 145, 149
Albert R., 23, 182, 193
Alexandrina, L., 82
Alice R., 143
Amadeus, L., 230
Arnheim B., 18
Austin, Mr. R., 240
Australia, why so called, 13
    Western, 97
    Crossing, 209, 210
    Centre of, 197, 201
Australis, Calamus, 146

Balonne R., 138
Barcoo R., 95, 143
Bass's Discoveries, 6-10
    Strait, 11, 12
Bathurst, Plains of, 30, 67-70
    Laid out, 36
Batman, John, 126
Baudin, 15
Belyando R., 142
Bight, Great Australian, 99-101, 221
Blacks— *see* Aborigines
Blaxland, Gregory, 28
Blue Mts., 25-33
    Unsuccessful attempt to cross, 25-27
    Crossed, 28-33
Bogan R., 71, 119-121
Botany B., 1
Bottle Trees, 139
Bourke, Fort, 121

Bridge, St. George's, 138
Brisbane R., 57
Broken B., 5
Burdekin R., 166
Burke, R. O'Hara, 168
    and Wills, 169-181
Byng, Mt., 134

Camels, 169, 213, 215, 218
Campaspe R., 134
Carpentaria, 135, 193
    Gulf of, 18, 173, 189
Castlereagh R., 42, 73
Condamine R., 154
Clark, George, *alias* "George the Barber," 111
Coal, Discovery of, 239
Cogoon R., 139
Convicts, 135
Cook, Capt., 1-3
Cooper's Ck., 93
Creek, Chambers's, 199
    Attack, 202
Cunningham, Allan, 53-65
    Richard, 119-120
    Gap, 63
Curtis B., 17

Danger Point, 2
Darling Downs, 60-61
    R., 71, 72, 80, 122, 137
Darwin, Port, 209
Dawson R., 154
Depôt Glen, 87
Desert, Gibson's, 233-234
Disappointment, Mt., 51
Droughts, 73, 74, 87

Eden, a new, 130
Encounter Bay, 15

Endeavour, ship, 1, 2
    R., 2
Essington, Port, 221
Eucla, Port, 221
Euryalean Scrub, 39
Evans, Surveyor, 34-36
Eyre, E. J., 85, 96-119
    Creek, 90

Falls, Alice, 232
Fawkner, J. P., 126
Farmer's Ck., 32
Finke, Mt., 196, 197
Fish R., 35
Fitzmaurice R., 23, 164
Fitzroy Downs, 139, 159
Fleet, First, 4
Flinders' Discoveries, 6-19
    R., 22, 23, 191, 193
Floods, Sudden, 137
Forrest, Hon. John, 219-228
Foxes, Flying, 156

Garden, Sydney Botanic, 63-64
George's R., 6
Giles, Ernest, 228-276
Gipps, Sir George, 153
Gosse, Mr., 225
Glenelg R., 132
Grampians, 132
Gregory, A. C., 163-166
Grey, Sir George, 237, 238

Hacking, Port, 7
Harris, Mt., 69
Hawkesbury R., 5
Hely, Hovenden, 161, 162
Henty, Edward, 125, 133
Hicks, Point, 1
Hastings R., 43
Hopeless, Mt., 177
Horses Poisoned, 240
Hovell, Capt., 47-52
Howitt, Alfred, 183-185
Hume, Hamilton, 46-52

Illawarra, 7
Iramoo Downs, 52
Isaacs, R. 155

Jackson, Port, 2
Jervis B., 8

Kangaroo Island, 14
    Grass, 129
    Rats, 155
Karaula R., 116
Kennedy, E. B., 135, 139, 144, 151
Kimberley, 242
Kindur R., 112
King, Governor, 16
    Admiral, 19-23
    Explorer, 171
    Found with the blacks, 184
Kites, Plague of, 155
Kyte, Ambrose, 167

Lachlan R., 35, 38-40
    Swamps, 39
Lakes, 131, 132, 185, 186
Landsborough, 182, 192, 193
Lang, Mt., 155
Lawson, William, 28
Leeuwin, Cape, 14
Leichhardt, 152-162, 220, 221
Liverpool Plains, 43
Loddon R., 129
Logan R., 61
Lynd R., 155

Macedon, Mt., 134
Mackenzie R., 154
Macquarie R., 35, 41, 42
    Port, 43
    Swamps, 41, 42, 70
Manning R., 44
Maranoa R., 139
Massacre, L., 186
M'Kinlay, John, 182, 185-189
Melbourne, 16
Menindie, 169
Mirage, 196
Mitchell, Sir Thomas, 80, 110-143
Moreton B., 154
Mosquitos, 207
Murchison R., 224
Murrumbidgee R., 48, 75
Murray R., 50, 77-84, 128, 134

Namoi R., 43, 115

INDEX.

Nardoo, 178, 186
New South Wales, why so called, 3
    Foundation of, 4
Nive R., 141
Nivelle R., 141
Nogoa R., 141
Norman R., 190, 191
    Captain, 182, 191

Oakover R., 215
Overlanding, 96
Oxley, John, 37-44, 69
    His Journal, 38
    His unfortunate prediction, 45

Palms, Glen of, 229
Pandora's Pass, 56
Petrel, Sooty, 10
Pillar, Chambers's, 199
Phillip, Port, 16
Plant, Poisonous, 240
Portland B., 133
Promise, Plains of, 23

Rawlinson Range, 233
Reef, Great Barrier, 17
Religion, Powerful support of, 238
Roe, J. S., 238, 239
Roper R., 206, 207
Rossiter B., 107
Rufus R., why so called, 82

Saltbush, 136, 137
Sea, Inland, supposed existence of, 42, 201
Seaview, Mt., 43
Shoalhaven, 8
Snowy Mts., 49
Soil, Poor, accounted for, 81
Sound, King George's, 107
" Spring " Country, 198
Squatters, Pioneer, 136, 159
Stapylton, L., 127
Stephens, Port, 44

Stokes, Capt., 23
Stony Desert, 90, 93, 94, 188
Strzelecki's Ck., 93
Stuart, John M'Douall, 194-209
    Central Mt., 201
Sturt, Capt., 66-95, 166
    Ck., 164
    Plains, 204
Sunday Services, 226
    Dinner, 226
Sydney Harbour, 4

Telegraph, Transcontinental, 209
Termination, L., 164
Territory, Northern, 209
Torrens, L., 98, 99, 195
Transportation, 3
Tumut R., 49
Twofold B., 9

Van Diemen's Land (Tasmania) circumnavigated, 10-12
Victoria, 125-135
    R., 23, 143, 163, 164, 202

Walker, Frederick, 182, 190-192
Warrego R., 141
Warburton, Colonel, 210-218
Warning, Mt., 2
Water, How found, 102, 103,
    Searching for, 213
    Subterranean, 243
    Caught during shower by tarpaulin, 213
Weld, Governor, 224
    Springs, 224
Wellington Valley, 40
Wells, Native, 213
Wentworth, W. C., 28
Western Port, 9
Wickham, Capt., 23
William, Mt., 131
Wills, W., 168, 169
Wimmera R., 131

Yass Plains, 47
York, Cape, 145

George Robertson and Co., Printers, Melbourne and Sydney.

www.ingramcontent.com/pod-product-compliance
Lightning Source LLC
Chambersburg PA
CBHW021353230426
43666CB00006B/508